Thinking T

General Editors
Graham Slater and C. S. Rodd

5. Is There Life After Death?

Thinking Things Through

Already Published

The Bible
C. S. Rodd

Worship
Michael J. Townsend

The Christian and People of Other Faiths
Peter D. Bishop

Why Evil and Suffering?
C. S. Rodd

In Preparation

The Sacraments
Michael J. Townsend

What To Do?
Richard G. Jones

Thinking Things Through

5. Is There Life After Death?

C. S. Rodd

EPWORTH PRESS

ISBN 0-7162-0520-3

First published 1998
by Epworth Press
20 Ivatt Way,
Peterborough
PE3 7PG

Typeset by the author
Printed and bound by
Biddles Ltd
Guildford and King's Lynn

Contents

Contents

General Introduction

The great German theologian, Hans Küng, has said that his aim in all his writings is to enable his readers to hold their faith with confidence and not with a bad conscience. This new series, prompted by the conviction that Christians need to think through their faith but often lack appropriate help in so doing, has a similar aim. Moreover, the assistance that it seeks to offer is related to another conviction: that many church members need persuading that theologians are concerned in any way with their problems and that theology can be at all relevant to their lives.

In such a situation, it is essential, we are sure, to begin with life and with church life. Only in that way can we be confident that we are dealing with grassroots issues. Plainly, however, it is not enough to identify the questions where they arise; we must also indicate the sources of help – if not of all the answers – in as non-technical a way as possible.

In some volumes, these tasks will be tackled in sequence; in others, they will be interwoven. Whatever the precise format, however, our hope is that, through this interaction, difficulties will be faced, fears dispelled, open discussion promoted, and faith informed and strengthened.

The books can either be read by individuals on their own or used in groups. We hope the questions at the end of each chapter will be useful both as a check that the text has been understood and as a spur to reflection and discussion.

Later volumes will deal with such issues as the sacraments, making moral decisions, Jesus, the Holy Spirit, creation and providence, salvation and discipleship, prayer, science and religion, and presenting the gospel.

GRAHAM SLATER AND C. S. RODD

Introduction

Everyone dies
Like an amateur,
For they know
No other way.

Some of those who pick up this book may feel that it is unnecessarily sceptical. I should perhaps explain, therefore, that its approach arises from an acceptance of two important, if uncomfortable, facts.

First, there is today more uncertainty about life after death than about almost any other part of the Christian faith, and the questioning is found as much within the churches as outside.

Second, ideas about life after death in the Bible are almost as diverse as those in circulation today. For much of the time covered by the Old Testament the Israelites held the *sheol* belief, which had no place for a happy future life with God. When belief in life after death did emerge, it was conceived in various ways, sometimes using the notion of 'resurrection', sometimes that of a more spiritual existence. Even in the New Testament, where a firm belief in life after death is found, there is a range of views about what exactly is to be expected.

Once again I am deeply grateful to Graham Slater for his co-operation over this series and especially for his constant encouragement during the time of writing this book. As with my earlier books, he has been a most enthusiastic supporter, and gentle but firm critic of my style. I am also grateful to Gerald Burt and G. W. S. Knowles for reading the text and offering perceptive and helpful comments. I must point out that I alone am responsible for the ideas expressed in it.

C. S. RODD

ix

Part 1

What Can We Believe?

1

A Happy Death

It was a peaceful and happy death. Mary's father, having spent most of the day working in his garden, and the evening reading and watching the television news, had gone to bed with his usual cheerful, 'Good night, my dear'; and when she went to wake him in the morning with his cup of tea she found that he had died in his sleep.

It was so different from her mother's death. She had become increasingly senile, until she didn't recognize her husband and daughter. The fact that she was incontinent, often wandered in the middle of the night, and was strong in body but with little mind left at all, put a tremendous strain on Mary's father. But he refused to allow her to go into a home. 'She is my wife', he said, and explained that he had taken a vow 'for better for worse ... in sickness and in health', and he wasn't going to break that vow. He was, he added, perfectly able to look after her – and did so with remarkable devotion and stamina. Mary used to say that when he looked at her mother he didn't see a senile old woman but the girl he had married so many years before. When she at last died Mary knew that all the members of her church were saying it was 'a happy release'. And she felt that in a way it was. But how would her father cope now? His whole life had been taken up with looking after her mother, doing as much as possible himself, and only calling on Mary to help him very occasionally. 'You have your own life to live,' he would say. 'You mustn't feel that you are tied to looking after us.' And it was he who insisted that she kept her own house and didn't move in with them.

Her father had been completely composed at the funeral and afterwards. 'She is with Jesus,' he said, 'and when I go to join her she will know me again.' He had been lonely. That was obvious. But it was the kind of loneliness of someone whose

3

wife is away on a holiday rather than of someone who had been bereaved.

Now he too had died. It was a tremendous loss to Mary. Since her mother's death she had made a point of staying with him every evening until he went to bed, and going in the morning to take him up a cup of tea. They lived quite near to each other and she knew that he wouldn't wish to give up his home, the home which he had shared with her mother for so long, the home he kept absolutely spotless, with the brass ornaments shining, and never a hint of dust or spiders' webs. So she never tried to persuade him to come to live with her. Now she found it very difficult to know what to say to those church members who tried to comfort her with 'He's with your mother now.' She knew it was her father's absolute conviction. And yet . . . She supposed that she wasn't a very good Christian, although she never missed church on Sunday. But she couldn't see how it was possible for life to continue after the body had died. Her mother's brain had decayed, destroying her personality. What was there left to live on?

At the graveside she longed to believe that that wasn't the end of her father. She had always been close to him, closer to him, perhaps, than to her mother, and he had remained the same father that she had always known, right up to his death. Even so, what could there be when the body decayed in the ground? She listened to the words that were so well intentioned, and hardly heard them. She felt somehow disloyal to her father. But she couldn't get away from that 'And yet . . .' Was there really any life after death?

In the days after the funeral she felt more lonely than she had thought was possible. There was no one now with whom in the evening she could share the news of the day. Each day began with no brightness and no purpose. Each day ended with silent grieving, made worse because she couldn't escape the thought that she might never see her parents again.

4

In the end she decided that she must talk to someone. She couldn't face those who were so triumphantly confident. She knew what a good man her father had been, and although it was a comfort to hear people say so, she wasn't helped by what to her seemed a facile assertion that he was in heaven. It was a different kind of consolation that she wanted. She needed to think things through – honestly and truthfully. There were only two people she knew she could trust to accept her as she was, loving yet disbelieving. They were Anne and Geoff.

Questions for discussion

1. Why did Mary feel that the comforting words spoken by the members of her church were facile? What kind of comfort do you think she needed?

2. How do you respond to Mary's view that there was no personality of her mother left to live on after her death?

3. Before reading any more chapters, try to set out what your own beliefs about life after death are.

2

Geoff Listens

Mary decided that she would go to see Geoff first. He was more confident than Anne, and although she wanted the truth, a bit of confidence would be helpful too. She knew he would understand how she felt and wouldn't run away from difficulties or pretend that they didn't exist. He would never try to cheer her up with platitudes that he knew she wouldn't believe.

When she arrived at the door of his flat he held her hand very firmly and pulled her gently in. 'Tea or coffee?' he asked, and bustled off to make the coffee. She sat and looked round his room. The pictures weren't religious, and yet there was something about them that she could only call spiritual. Everything was neat and tidy, and yet the room looked as if it was lived in. By the time Geoff came in with the coffee she was already feeling more composed.

They sat together for quite a long time in silence. Yet it wasn't an embarrassed silence. Geoff seemed to know that, though she valued his company, she needed space to be quiet for a while. The evening sunset began to fade and Geoff turned on the lights and drew the curtains. It was that drawing of the curtains that brought a catch to her throat. The remaining daylight was now shut out.

'Yes,' Geoff said, 'the day comes to an end. Now tell me about your father.' Once she had started to speak, Mary found that she could tell him about her feelings and her doubts very easily. She wasn't a very good Christian, was she? Hardly a Christian at all. Her father had had such a firm, joyful faith. He never doubted for one moment that he would meet her mother again. He pictured heaven very much as a continuation of life on earth – without the sorrows, without the illness, above all, without her mother's loss of mind and memory. Mary repeated to Geoff that phrase that summed up his faith for her:

6

'She is with Jesus, and when I go to join her she will know me again.'

'But I just can't believe that,' she said. And there was silence again.

After a little while Geoff said, very quietly, 'Tell me what you do believe.' To Mary it seemed a strange thing to say. She had been telling herself that she just didn't believe at all: that she had never had much faith and that now she had lost what little she had had. What did she believe? There was silence again. How glad she was that Geoff didn't put on a record as background music. Silence was what she needed.

At last she said, 'I don't know.' Again she stopped, but this time there seemed to be a compulsion to say something. What did she believe? She believed that her father was the best man she had ever known. She believed that his faith was sincere and she longed to have that kind of faith. But somehow it just wouldn't come. She went to church as regularly as she had done before her father died. It was partly out of loyalty to him, but partly because she had hoped that by going to church she would find his kind of faith. But it hadn't worked out like that. She found the well-intended words of the other church members irritating, not comforting. When she listened to the Bible readings sometimes they reminded her of her father's faith and sometimes their very beauty eased her sorrow. But the hymns seemed to come from a distant world and to have nothing to say to her. That was why she had come to see Geoff.

After another long pause, she said: 'When I was about nine my father took me to see Peter Pan. I don't remember much about it now, apart from the children flying, and coming right out over the audience. But there's one thing I have never been able to forget. It was at that point when Tinkerbell drinks the poison intended for Peter Pan and her light begins to fade. All the children in the audience are told that the only thing that can save her is to say that they believe in fairies. I remember very well how loudly all the children shouted out, "Yes", when Peter

7

Pan asked them if they did. But I was silent. I wanted Tinkerbell to live, but I just couldn't shout out what I didn't believe. It's rather like that with father. I long to believe that he and mother are happy together again now, but I just can't. And it makes me feel as if I'm destroying his faith as well as my own.'

She stopped, and Geoff said, 'And what do you believe about death?' She was immensely glad that he had said the word. It enabled her to tell him what she really thought. It came out in rather a jumble, and it was only after Geoff had put it together for her that she came to understand where she stood.

She couldn't imagine what life in heaven could be like. How it was possible for anyone to be alive without their bodies. As her mother became more and more senile, she became less and less the mother that she had known. The gracious, happy, confident mother who could always be relied upon wasn't there. Conversation with her had become quite impossible. She didn't know any of them any more. She wasn't really a person at all. There was no 'soul' to go to heaven. She was just a body with a brain that had worn out. What was there to live on in an afterlife?

With her father it was different. It was fairly easy to imagine him continuing to live on just as he was the evening before he had died. But that was to suppose that heaven was the continuation of life here on earth, and life on earth depends upon bodies, and clothes, and food and all the other things that make up living. That is the only way we know our friends. We talk to each other, and that means possessing tongues and ears and living in a world with air to carry the sound. What could life in heaven possibly mean?

She wondered what picture of heaven her father had had. When he said that her mother would know him, was he imagining the time when they were both young and in love for the first time? Or was it the time before the dread disease had struck and the three of them were a happy family? Whatever it

8

was she was sure that he was simply looking back to one of the happy times in his life and imagining that going on for ever. And that just couldn't be true.

By the time she had said all this in her faltering way it was quite late. Geoff had simply said, 'Perhaps the biggest problem that we all have about life after death is that we can't imagine what it can be like. I wonder whether we need to stop trying to picture it and think first of all about some of the things that have made Christians believe that God has a future stored away for us.'

Mary was glad that he had said that, and went home a little calmer than she had been for a long time. She was especially glad that Geoff had said so little and encouraged her to talk. It had been a comfort to be able just to tell someone what she really believed. At church she had had to pretend all the time and hide her doubts. She was particularly pleased that he was going to come round to her home for coffee so that they could talk about it a bit more.

Before they could have that talk, however, Easter came. It made a great difference to several people in her church, especially to Anne, and it made Mary think out her ideas more deeply.

Questions for discussion

1. How do you picture heaven?

2. What do you believe about people who suffer from Alzheimer's disease?

3. What other problems about life after death does Mary's reaction to the death of her parents raise?

3

This Joyful Eastertide

It had been a wonderful Easter. Chris and Steve, two art teachers, had transformed the whole front of the church into an Easter garden, and when the minister proclaimed, 'The Lord is risen,' the response of the large congregation, 'He is risen indeed,' sounded out as a great affirmation of faith. Anne left the service with Hallelujahs ringing in her ears.

On Wednesday the church had again been full for George's funeral. George was over eighty and was well known and well liked both within the church and in the local community. 'A fine Christian character', was how everyone described him. The minister said that, if we could choose the moment of our death, no time would be more appropriate for the Christian than Easter. They had sung the Easter hymn again, with its line, 'Made like him, like him we rise'. It all fitted together so wonderfully: the triumph of the resurrection and the confidence in life with Christ for the Christian. Anne was sad that George would never be in his familiar place in the church again. She would miss his cheery word to her, but this didn't seem to be a time for grief. He had lived out his life as a true follower of Christ, and Christ's resurrection would surely be his.

The mood of joy appeared to be echoed in the weather. The weeks of dull skies, cold and frequent rain had come to an end at last. Easter Day was the first for several weeks when the sun shone in clear blue skies. The birds sang and the daffodils gleamed brightly by the side of the roads, on roundabouts, and in the front gardens of the houses she passed on her way to church. And the good weather continued all the week.

On the next Sunday, however, the preacher had made Anne think. He said that on Easter Day they had all offered to God the worship of their hearts. Now it was time to give him the worship of their minds, and he wanted to open up some thoughts about the resurrection. He referred to a modern theologian who had said that we must be men and women of the twentieth century who want to believe in the resurrection not half heartedly, with a bad conscience, but honestly and with conviction. This meant that we must face up to the difficulties and not be satisfied with an emotional faith.

Yes, that was certainly true. She had been carried along all week by the thrill of that Easter Day service. But she knew that she couldn't be satisfied with 'spiritual uplift'. That wasn't her style. It might be sufficient for some people, and sometimes she envied their exuberance, but she had to think things through. Geoff might call her a little worrier (the way he said it was never patronizing – there was always a twinkle in his eye), but she found that once she had seen a problem she had to work it out and find the answer. It had been like that with the Bible. To face up to the difficulties that were there meant that her faith was firmer now than it had been. And how much more meaning she now found in the readings in the services than she had ever seen before.

She had missed the first part of the sermon thinking about all this, and was suddenly surprised when she heard the preacher saying that it was unlikely that the empty tomb was part of the earliest Christian message about the resurrection. He pointed to Paul, who listed all the people to whom Jesus had appeared, including himself, and didn't mention the empty tomb at all. He said that he personally believed that the body of Jesus decayed exactly like our bodies will. The resurrection wasn't a matter of a corpse coming back to life again, but was something quite different and completely new. Jesus had been raised from the dead into a new kind of life. We should pay more attention to what Paul said than to the stories at the end of the Gospels. Paul was convinced that Jesus was alive, not because of an empty tomb, but because he had met Jesus himself. The preacher pointed out that this didn't make the resurrection any less real. He fully believed in the resurrection; indeed, he

11

believed in it more confidently than he would have done if he had had to accept that the body of Jesus had been brought back to life again. Jesus was alive today. That was what mattered for our faith.

After the service Anne had asked the preacher whether he could still sing the Easter hymns. He replied immediately, 'Of course'. Some of the words might belong to an earlier age, but he had just the same faith in the resurrection that the writers had, even though he would express it rather differently.

Fred had been upset after the service. 'So you don't really believe that Jesus rose from the dead,' he had said to the preacher. 'You think it was just hallucinations. Jesus really was dead in the tomb.' And he hadn't been satisfied when the preacher had tried to explain that he did believe in the resurrection, but not in the resuscitation of his dead body. For Fred, unless Jesus came back to life again in a real body of flesh and blood, he wasn't raised.

Anne was troubled. Did Jesus rise from the dead or not? If the Easter faith was based on the appearances of Jesus to the disciples, in what way were those appearances different from visions? All sorts of people claimed to have had visions. Many Catholic women had had visions of the Virgin Mary, but when Protestants had visions it was Jesus and never Mary whom they saw. Could you really rely on visions, when you saw what you expected to see? That Easter garden that Chris and Steve had constructed in the church had focussed on the empty tomb. If the preacher was right, that didn't lie at the heart of the Easter message. And did he really have the same faith as the writers of those Easter hymns? Or was he simply deceiving himself when he thought that his faith was the same as theirs?

And there was George. The resurrection of Jesus gave the assurance that George was still alive too. And all those other members of her church who had died recently. She thought of Mary's father, and the confidence he had had that when he died he would meet his beloved wife again. What if the body of

Jesus hadn't been raised after all? What if the disciples had just imagined that Jesus had appeared to them? What if those appearances of Jesus were hallucinations? She knew of a friend who had told her that for several months after her husband died she kept on imagining that she was seeing him – in the supermarket when she was doing the shopping, or sitting in his chair.

Anne wanted to be a twentieth-century woman, and she also wanted to believe in the resurrection honestly and with conviction. She would have to read the Gospels again. And she would have to talk it over with Geoff.

Anne thought about it as she walked home. She had learnt enough about the Bible now to know that we have to make a long journey to a foreign time in order to understand it. And she had lost all her anxieties about making that journey. She had discovered that she wasn't worried any more that we can never be completely certain about any of the words of Jesus. Even so, wasn't the resurrection rather different?

And there was still that hymn that they had sung. 'Made like him, like him we rise'. What if his body had decayed in the ground? And if the resurrection of Jesus wasn't the coming back to life again of someone who had died but was something completely different, then was it really true that we should rise like him?

Questions for discussion

1. How do you respond to what the preacher said? What do you believe about the resurrection of Jesus?

2. In what ways is it possible to distinguish between the appearances of Jesus to the disciples as recorded in the Gospels and hallucinations?

3. Consider whether belief in human life after death depends upon believing in the resurrection of Jesus.

4

Anne and Mary Share their Doubts

It was a beautiful spring afternoon and Mary was glad that
Anne had suggested that they should go for a walk together
along the shore. They watched the waders on the mud and
listened to the skylark's song and the strange, mysterious cry of
the curlew – and were thoroughly enjoying themselves until
they reached that part of the path that went through the
cemetery. The path took them by the side of the rows of
children's graves. There were more now than when Mary had
gone that way before. For a time the two friends were silent.
Then Mary spoke. 'I find it terribly depressing to come along
here. I don't know why the council put all the children's graves
together.' 'I suppose it's because they think it helps the
parents,' Anne replied. 'They don't feel alone, and get comfort
from one another.' 'I'm still not sure,' said Mary. 'Just think of
all these small children who have died. Look, a baby only a few
weeks old. A little boy of six. A tiny girl, with a teddy bear on
the grave as well as a mass of flowers. That grave with the
dinosaur toys.'

She stopped suddenly. Anne put her arm round her shoulders
and led her to a seat. They were quiet for a long time, and then
Mary said, 'I'm sorry. It just came over me. All these parents
hope that one day they will see their children again in heaven.
Look at the inscriptions. But I can't imagine how that is
possible.'

Anne spoke quietly. 'Tell me.'

'I can't get away from thinking of those parents,' Mary said.
'What strange ideas they seem to have. One gravestone says
that God lent Robin to them for three years. Another declares
that God needed an angel and took Ann. There's even one that
speaks of Christina waiting for them in heaven. Another says
that Alison was a bud on earth and is now a flower in heaven.
Most of them seem to imagine that their children will remain

just as they were on earth. Robin will always be a three-year-old boy. Ann will be an angel, but I'm sure they think of her as a child angel. And they talk about Christina as if they'd been out for the day and when they come back she will be at the door to welcome them home. Only the parents of Alison suggest that she will be "grown up" in heaven.'

After that they had a long talk. Anne wondered how else the parents could possibly imagine their children. Mary pointed out that the parents would change. They would certainly grow older and any other children they already had or would have later on would grow older as well. Sadly some of the parents would get divorced. They might remarry and have other children. All their relationships would be quite different. When they eventually died they would be different people, not as they were on the day that Robin, Ann, Christina, and Alison had died. And they might feel quite differently about their children.

All this worried Anne. She looked across the cemetery and noticed the war memorial. Binyon's well-known words came into her mind:

> They shall grow not old, as we that are left grow old:
> Age shall not weary them, nor the years condemn.

'I suppose,' she said, 'what we all treasure is the memory of our loved ones as we knew them. We have the memories, and the family photograph album. Some will have videos in which those who have died will still move about and talk and laugh.' And then she was suddenly silent. How callous it seemed to talk to Mary like that. After all, she hadn't recently lost a father as Mary had. But Mary turned to her and smiled. 'Thank you for saying that,' she said. 'I wish everyone would talk to me honestly and not be embarrassed or feel they must treat me like a child.'

They got up and continued their walk. The sun still shone. The skylarks still sang. But the world had grown grey for them. Mary was thinking about her father – and her mother. Anne was remembering the Easter Day service and what the preacher had said the following Sunday. Was a memory all that was left, after all?

Questions for discussion

1. Anne wondered how else the parents of children who had died could think about their children except as they were – children. How do you picture the future life of children who have died?

2. Mary found changing family relationships made it very difficult for her to believe in a life after death in which we meet our loved ones. Think about your own changing relationships. How does this affect your ideas of a future life?

5

Trying to Put it All Together

Mary told Anne that Geoff was coming round for a chat about some of the problems she had with life after death, and invited her to join them.

Over coffee they told Geoff about their walk through the cemetery and how upset it had made both of them. He listened in his usual quiet way as they spoke about the dead children and the war memorial, and then he said: 'It's a real problem, and I don't know the answer.' He looked at Mary. 'It's the same problem that we talked about before Easter. We find it so difficult to imagine any kind of existence that is different from the one we know. If we can't really imagine how homeless people feel, or what kind of life the Queen really lives, is it any wonder that we can't imagine what life in heaven is like?'

Mary wasn't satisfied. 'I can see that,' she said, 'but that is only a small part of my problem. What I find difficult is to understand what meeting our relatives and friends in heaven can possibly mean. If we all died on the same day it might make sense. But we all go on living after one of our loved ones has died. And that means that we change. I remember a television presenter who commented after a story of two young sweethearts who had gone their own ways and then met again by chance after over thirty years and decided to get married: "We'll keep you up to date with the divorce"! I shouldn't be at all surprised if it happened. They weren't the same people as they were when they were twenty.'

'That's true,' Geoff said, 'but it doesn't mean that life after death makes no sense, does it? You are supposing that life in heaven is simply continuing life on earth – though without the pain and the partings. But how can it be? Our life is material. We have bodies and it is through those bodies that we meet our friends. In heaven we shall be changed. Meeting one another will be different.'

17

Anne was even more worried about this idea. 'If we're changed,' she said, 'how shall we recognize each other? I met a college friend not long ago and didn't know who she was. It was most embarrassing. She seemed to know me, which made it worse. What I mean is, that if we don't recognize each other because we have grown older and look different from what we did twenty-five years ago, how can we possibly know each other in heaven where we don't have bodies?'

Mary then repeated the question that she had asked Geoff before. 'What is there to survive death?' Her mother's mind was destroyed and she wasn't the mother she had once known. Her father imagined her in heaven as she was when she was young, but that wasn't how she actually was when she died.

Geoff was silent for quite a long time, and then he said: 'The answer that many people will give you is that it's your mother's soul that is reunited with your father's soul in heaven. But I find it difficult to accept that. I expect both of you do as well.'

Anne and Mary nodded. Even though they didn't want to believe it, they were both convinced that our minds give us the only 'personality' we have. When the brain decays, that is the end. What would a 'soul' mean? All three friends began to put forward problems about the idea of an immortal soul. How was it related to the brain? Didn't medical research show that our thoughts and emotions were all affected by what went on between the cells of the brain? If there were souls, was each soul individually created by God? Or were they literally immortal, and had lived – elsewhere – before they were joined to particular men and women? But in either case, how could this be reconciled with the evolution of human beings?

Geoff pointed out that it was precisely because of these difficulties that many people today rejected the idea of the soul and held that human beings were single wholes, composed of the bodies that we know. When we die, that is the end of our body; and if there is to be any future life, it must be through a miracle. God will have to 'raise us from the dead', in the same way that Jesus was raised. He added that he himself wasn't too sure about this.

Anne was intrigued, and urged him to say more.

'It's like this,' he said. 'Suppose John Smith died and another John Smith appeared in Australia, looking and acting and thinking *exactly* like the John Smith who had died, could we say that it *was* John Smith? Wouldn't it be just a replica, an imitation of the original John Smith? A clone? Isn't this what is implied in talking about a resurrection. God creates a replica in heaven. He can't do anything else, because the human being who died has ceased to exist. There is nothing to 'carry over' from the present life to the future life.'

'So I'm right', said Mary sadly. 'Death *is* the end. We must just accept it and live our lives fighting it as long as we can and making the most of the life we have. I don't mean that we should live for the day. Making the most of our life might mean devoting ourselves to assist other people. But we must reconcile ourselves to the fact that this life is all.'

'Not necessarily,' Geoff replied, 'but I think that any alternative is going to be very difficult to imagine.' '"Imagine" again', laughed Anne. 'You think it is all a matter of our feeble imaginations, don't you?' 'Not entirely,' said Geoff, 'but I think that imagination has a lot to do with it.'

He went on: 'Some people have suggested that we might think of life after death as a computer program. It exists only in the hardware, in the disk or in the computer memory chips, yet it can be transferred from one computer to another. In the same way the individual can be passed from a human body to a spiritual existence in heaven.'

Anne looked puzzled. 'I shall have to think about that,' she said, 'but I feel in my bones that there is something not quite right about it.'

Is There Life After Death?

Questions for discussion

1. Two separate ideas of life after death have been considered here: an immortal soul and a resurrection. What is the difference between them? Which is the way you have thought about life after death?

2. The discussion in this chapter has raised a lot of questions about both the immortal soul and a resurrection. Which do you think are the most difficult to answer? How would you set about answering them?

3. Anne said she needed to think about Geoff's model of life after death as a computer program, but she felt something was wrong with it. What have you to say about it?

4. How important is a belief in life after death for the Christian? What difference would it make if death *were* the end?

6

Hell

The next Sunday morning the preacher offended several devout members of the congregation and Fred tackled her after the service.

'So you don't believe what our Lord has told us,' he said. The preacher wasn't surprised by the question. When she wrote her sermon she knew that some people in her congregation would disagree with what she was going to say, but she believed that it was important to set out a true picture of God as she understood it.

The Gospel reading was Mark 9.38–50, in which Jesus said that if our hand or eye causes us to sin, it would be better to cut it off or tear it out rather than to be thrown into hell 'where the fire is never quenched'. In her sermon the preacher had boldly talked about hell. She said outright that she didn't believe that God ever punished anyone with everlasting torment in a fiery hell. That would be quite contrary to justice. Today we expect the punishment to be related to the crime that has been committed. It would be outrageous to torture anyone for ever, even for the most terrible of crimes. It would also be out of character for God. How could we suppose that a God who was a loving Father would do that? Indeed, Jesus didn't actually threaten everlasting punishment. He only said that the fire in hell wouldn't be put out, not that sinners would have to live in it for ever.

She went on to say that she accepted that we can't know what will happen to any of us after death. Perhaps wicked people will simply cease to exist. Perhaps eventually everyone will respond to God's love and be 'saved', however long it may take. Perhaps God's love will never be able to win them back, and because God refuses to force anyone to be good against their will, those who hate goodness and don't want to be

21

reconciled to God will be separated from him for ever – and that is what hell is. They will shut themselves out of heaven. What we can be certain of is that God is a loving God and he won't inflict the kind of punishments that we would condemn if human beings punished anyone in that way. To think that God will thrust anyone into an everlasting hell is to malign him. She quoted the great nineteenth-century scholar, E. B. Pusey, one of the leaders of the Oxford Movement: 'You know the fierce, intense, burning, heat of a furnace, how it consumes in a moment anything cast into it. Its misery to the damned shall be that they feel it, but can't be consumed by it. The fire shall pierce them, penetrate them; it shall be, Scripture says, like a molten "lake of fire", rolling, tossing, immersing, but not destroying.' 'How can a Christian believe anything like that today?' she asked.

Anne and several other members of the congregation gathered round to see how the preacher would answer Fred. She explained that she believed that Jesus was a man of his own time. Many people at that time believed in a heaven in the sky and in a hell under the earth. They really did believe that sinners would literally be cast into hell. Jesus simply accepted the ideas that were current in his own day. What *we* have to do is to think out how we suppose the God we believe in will treat evil men and women.

Fred's response was firm. 'But Jesus is the Son of God. If he said that sinners would be punished by being sent to everlasting fire, that is sufficient for me. And he didn't say it just once. Remember the parable about the Rich Man and Lazarus (Luke 16.19–31). If you don't accept what Jesus said, you don't really believe that he was the Son of God.'

The preacher quietly explained that she *did* believe that Jesus was the Son of God (Anne felt sure that she would interpret this in a rather different way from Fred). But Jesus was also human, and that meant that he grew up believing many things that other people at the time believed.

22

Hell

Fred wasn't convinced. He could see, he said, that Jesus didn't know anything about television or aircraft. Here Alec, one of the other members of the congregation butted in. 'If he was God, he must have known about all the modern inventions. It was just that he didn't speak about them because he knew the people wouldn't understand.' Fred replied he wouldn't go as far as that. But the point he wanted to make was this: Jesus mightn't have known about some scientific things, but he knew everything about God and about salvation. When he said that sinners would be consigned to hell, he was telling us what will actually happen if we don't believe in his sacrifice on the cross.

The preacher realized that she and Fred weren't going to persuade each other, and she simply said: 'What matters to me is the kind of God I believe in. I can't believe in a God who would send anyone to everlasting torture. Look at it like this,' she said. 'You surely don't think it would be right to imprison those two boys who killed James Bulger, and then torture them every day for the rest of their lives. Even in America where they execute murderers they do it as painlessly as possible. We mustn't make God worse than we are in our best moments.'

Alec had a ready answer to this. 'My thoughts are not your thoughts, neither are your ways my ways, saith the Lord,' he quoted. The Bible clearly says that we can only be saved through the name of Jesus. I've no time for those people who suppose that they will be given a second chance after they have died. There is nothing in the Bible about that. They can repent right up till their last breath, but after that comes the judgment.' Fred was troubled. He didn't want to contradict Alec, but he would have liked to believe that everyone would repent in the end.

Suddenly Mrs Smith spoke. 'I think we need a hell,' she said. 'Life is just too unfair. Good people suffer, rogues and criminals get away with it. Where's the justice if they don't reap their reward after they're dead?' Everyone knew that Mrs Smith spoke from bitter experience. He husband had been

23

killed by a drunken driver. One of her daughters had been raped and strangled. And she had struggled to bring up six children. The driver was given a fine and banned from driving for two years. The rapist was never caught.

Anne was thinking about all this and missed the first words of the preacher's reply. When she came to, she heard the preacher explaining that she didn't for one moment wish to say that there would be no judgment. She was only concerned that the punishment itself should be just. She also felt that, if we placed too much emphasis upon rewards in heaven, we might fail to work to correct the injustices in society here and now.

At this Mary spoke up. 'You speak of judgment as if it were an English Crown Court. But whatever kind of life there may be after death, it can't be just like life in England. Even today other countries have different legal systems. Life after death must be so different that we just can't imagine what it is like. In any case I believe that God is better than the very best people we have ever known, not worse.'

Ron, who had been listening quietly to the discussion up to this point, now spoke. 'All this speculation may be very interesting to you,' he said, 'but it really doesn't matter one little bit to me. I'm not at all concerned to find out what happens after death. I believe that the God who is the Father of Jesus loves us, and that's all I need to know. I can't imagine what life may be like beyond death, and I don't want to try. When Isobel died I committed her to God's love. I trust him. That's all there is to it. We can't know. We can only respond to God's love.' He paused and they were all silent. Then he added, 'Like Mary, I believe that God is better than the best people we have ever known. And that means that he loves Isobel in just the same way that I did, and still do. But his love is even stronger and more tender.' Again he paused. 'The heart of the matter for me is this. If we have known the love and care of God in this life, then we may surely trust him for what lies beyond death.'

As she walked home Anne was thoughtful. Much of the discussion seemed unreal to her. The preacher, Fred, and Alec obviously believed that after we die we continue to be just the same kind of people that we are now. And so did Mrs Smith, come to that. That was what she found so difficult to accept. If we survive as 'souls' – spirit beings of some kind – we wouldn't have 'bodies'; and it is only through our bodies that we think and feel and know one another. If God gives new life to the dead in some kind of 'resurrection', they still won't have physical bodies. It was quite impossible to believe in dead bodies being brought back to physical life. But really she found it difficult to imagine any kind of future life after we had died. She could sympathize with Fred, because she knew how much he loved his Bible and his Lord. In the discussion, however, her feelings had been on the side of the preacher. Yet she couldn't see what 'person' there was to be sent to hell – or to go to heaven, for that matter.

And Alec's comments troubled her. God certainly was so much greater than she could possibly imagine that his thoughts were bound to be different from her thoughts. She wished people wouldn't talk so often as if they knew exactly what God was thinking. But it seemed to her to be quite another thing to say that cruelty could be part of his idea of goodness.

She wished she had the calm faith and serene trust that Ron showed.

Questions for Discussion

1. Which of the six people represents most closely your own ideas about hell: the preacher, Fred, Alec, Mary, Ron, or Anne? Try to explain more fully why you hold this belief.

2. As Mark reports the words of Jesus, Jesus believed in hell. How does this affect your belief about Jesus? (Look up also Luke 16.19–31.)

3. The preacher suggested three other ways of thinking about the fate of the wicked than assigning them to hell: (i) those who are wicked may cease to exist after death; (ii) the wicked refuse to accept God's love and so separate themselves from the happiness of fellowship with him; (iii) the wicked are given a 'second chance' after death, and in fact all will be eventually saved. Can you think of any other possible ways of escaping the idea of everlasting punishment? Why do you hold the beliefs about hell that you do?

4. Alec quoted Isaiah 55.8. Anne didn't believe that God's 'goodness' could be different from our ideas of goodness. How does this affect your beliefs about hell? (Look up Isaiah 55 and see whether Alec was using the text correctly.)

5. What do you think about the idea that a judgment and retribution after death is needed to correct the injustices of the life?

6. Ron had no desire to try to imagine what happened after death. Consider whether he is being realistic or is avoiding questions which raise doubts in his mind.

7

The Preacher Joins Geoff's Friends

Geoff arranged for Allison, who had preached that sermon on hell, to come to his flat and he invited Anne, Mary, Fred, Alec, and a friend whom none of the others had met before, Lesley, who, they discovered, taught in one of the new universities. Anne was surprised to see Janice as well. Janice had said very firmly on one occasion that she couldn't stand discussions about religion. She knew what she believed and for her religion was too personal a thing to discuss with other people. She looked across at Anne. 'Don't think I'm going to take part,' she said, with a grin. 'But I'm interested in what you people say about life after death. So I'm just going to sit and listen. Don't you dare ask me to tell you what I think.'

Geoff started things off. 'Your sermon certainly made us all think, Allison,' he said, 'and we are all so glad that you have come to talk it over with us. I think Anne wants to start off with something that has been troubling her.'

Anne explained that the sermon and the conversation afterwards had seemed rather unreal to her, since she couldn't see how there could be any 'person' to be sent to heaven or hell after death. 'We all seem to be assuming that life after death will simply be a continuation of life on earth, and I don't think it can be.'

Before Alec could say, 'So you don't believe what the Bible says, either!' Geoff turned to Lesley. 'We need your help, I think.'

'You won't want me to give a lecture,' said Lesley, laughing, 'but perhaps I could make a few simple points. I think we need to be clear about the Old Testament first of all. The surprising thing is that for most of the Old Testament period the Israelites didn't believe in a happy life after death. They thought the dead went into a kind of dark, underground hole where they were unable to have any contact with God and they gradually

27

became weaker and weaker. The woman of Tekoa said to David: "We must all die; we are like water spilled on the ground, which cannot be gathered up" (II Samuel 14.14). It was only in the very latest books of the Old Testament that beliefs in life after death appeared, and then it was expressed as "resurrection". So we have in the book of Daniel: "Many of those who sleep in the dust of the earth shall awake, some to everlasting life, and some to shame and everlasting contempt" (Daniel 12.2). That was probably written in about 164 BC.

'As you know, in the time of Jesus the Sadducees didn't believe in life after death. They told a story about a woman who had been married to seven brothers in turn to show how stupid ideas about it were (Mark 12.18–23). But by then many people *did* believe in a future life. The Pharisees did – and of course so did Jesus. But in his reply to the Sadducees Jesus made it clear that the resurrection life will be quite different from life on earth (Mark 12.24–27).

'What I think all this shows,' she added, 'is that it was perfectly possible to worship God and yet believe that death is the end. Perhaps we should remember that.'

Alec immediately butted in. 'I'm a Christian, and Christianity has superseded the Jewish religion. It doesn't matter what they believed in the Old Testament. The message of Jesus is that there is a resurrection, and after that a judgment, and everyone will then be sent to heaven or hell. The trouble with so many people today,' he added, 'is that they don't believe the Bible and won't accept what Jesus said. He made it quite clear that those who believe in him will be saved. He told the thief beside him on the cross that he would be with him in paradise that very day (Luke 23.43). He told his disciples that he was going to prepare a place for them in his Father's house, and that he would come and take them to be with him (John 14.1–3). But he also told the parable of the Sheep and the Goats (Matthew 25.31–45). And don't forget that the wicked in that parable go to eternal punishment. That's good enough for me.'

It looked as if things were going to get a bit tricky, and Fred tried to calm things down. 'As you know,' he said, 'I love Jesus and I take him at his word. But there are still things in the Gospels that puzzle me. I find it hard to understand what Jesus meant when he said that one day he will appear and gather his chosen ones from the ends of the earth to the ends of the heaven (Mark 13.26–27). There are a lot of things in the Bible I don't understand,' he added. 'I just trust him to look after me and my loved ones. I don't think we were meant to know what it is going to be like. We must just trust him.'

'That was partly my point,' Allison said, 'but I would put it in a different way. There are many things in the New Testament that we don't understand because the people in the time of Jesus thought differently from the way we think. And as I said in my sermon, Jesus was a man of his own age, not a twentieth-century man. And I think that the other thing that I said is just as important. We mustn't make God a worse person than we are in our best moments. For the rest I'm prepared to be agnostic. Like Fred, I'm willing simply to trust God.'

'But it isn't quite as easy as that, is it?' said Anne. 'Take those texts that Alec and Fred quoted. They are inconsistent. Jesus told the thief on the cross that they would be together in paradise straight away after they had died, but in the parable there is an elaborate judgment scene. Jesus told the disciples that he was going to prepare a place for them, but he also told the disciples that he was going to appear one day to gather his chosen ones. And how can you fit the resurrection into this? Was he really dead from Good Friday to Easter Day, and then was raised from the dead, or did his soul return to God when he died on the cross. And don't forget that he told the Sadducees that life in heaven would be quite different from life on earth.'

Allison admitted that she found this difficult too, but she thought that people in the time of Jesus were just as confused about life after death as we are today, and that this was why there were so many different ideas floating around. Some

29

people probably expected a resurrection to an unending life on earth. Some thought of a resurrection of the spirit, but not of the body. Some seem to have thought that the dead 'slept' until the final judgment, while others supposed that God's assessment takes place during our lives so that, when he dies, the poor man in the parable of the Rich Man and Lazarus is carried immediately by the angels to Abraham's bosom.

Mary wondered how Catholic teaching fitted into this. She had a colleague at work who was a Catholic and he believed that after we die we sleep until the day of judgment and then those who are saved go first to purgatory to be purified and fitted for heaven. That was why he prayed regularly for his parents and his sister who had died. Alec said that as a Protestant he couldn't accept that. It was quite clear that the final judgment takes place at the moment of death. 'So the people who died in that plane crash,' Geoff mused, 'were sent to heaven or hell at that moment, whereas if the plane hadn't crashed they would have had the rest of their lives before the judgment took place. Seems a bit arbitrary to me.'

'Can I raise something quite different?' said Anne. Last time Geoff discussed all this with Mary and me, Mary said that she couldn't really think of persons apart from their bodies and that death seemed to be the end. Geoff suggested that 'souls' were rather like a computer program. I found that puzzling. I wonder what Lesley has to say about it.'

'I'm not the oracle,' said Lesley, laughing. 'I'm really just as puzzled about all this as you are. But I can't really think that I'm just a brain in a body. There is a real "me". I'm not just a bundle of desires and feelings. I certainly can't think of myself as just a set of electric impulses in the brain. But I don't find the computer program at all helpful. The computer program after all may be transferred to different types of hardware but they are all the same in that they can store the electro-magnetic patterns. To suggest that in some way the human personality can be transferred to a 'soul' or a 'spiritual body' would be like

30

transferring a computer program to a cat's brain.' They all laughed, but Geoff said, 'I still think it's worth thinking about. No analogy fits exactly, otherwise it wouldn't be an analogy. I think that all that the computer illustration tries to do is to suggest that there is something about a human personality which God can "transfer" to a different kind of existence.'

'That reminds me of one of my friends at work,' said Anne. 'She's a Hindu and she believes that we have all lived many lives in the past as different people and that we shall continue to go on living as different people in the future until we have worked out the consequences of our good and bad deeds – I think she called it our *karma*. What do you think about that idea?'

'Rubbish', Alec retorted. 'There's nothing about reincarnation in the Bible. It's just a part of the pagan religion that we send our missionaries to convert the pagans from.'

Again Geoff needed all his powers of conciliation. 'I agree that there's nothing in the Bible,' he said, 'but can we simply write off the ideas that deeply religious people of other faiths hold? Shouldn't we at least try to understand what lies behind their beliefs?'

Fred tried to help Geoff out. 'As you all know,' he said, 'I love my Master and base my faith on my Bible, but that doesn't stop me from being puzzled quite often. I can't see anything desperately wrong in the idea that one life is too short for what we do in it to affect our eternal destiny. I don't believe in reincarnation, mind you,' he quickly added, looking at Alec, 'but I think we ought at least to think about it.'

'After all,' said Anne, feeling rather timid about saying anything in case it upset Alec again, 'if we believe in a soul, I don't really see why that soul shouldn't inhabit another body. But then, I find it difficult to see what the idea of a soul can mean. And if there really is reincarnation, why don't we remember anything about our past lives?'

'There's one other idea that I would like to throw in for you to think about,' Lesley said. 'One scholar has suggested that we shall continue to exist in God's memory.' 'That isn't what we find in the Bible,' Alec retorted. 'Jesus said that we shall continue to live with him in heaven as real people.' Even Geoff was a little put out. 'I don't think I want to be no more than a memory,' he said. Lesley tried to explain. 'The scholar realized that simply to say that God will remember us is far from being what Christians have always understood by eternal life. He stressed that he was using memory only as an analogy. The idea he wants to put across is that the past is still present with God in a very lively and realistic way. We shan't remain fixed and unchanged for ever in God's memory, like a fly caught centuries ago in amber or a mammoth preserved in a glacier.' It was such a novel idea that the others weren't sure what to think about it. Anne wondered how the past could possibly be changed, even in the mind of God. 'I'm afraid it's beyond me,' Fred admitted. 'I shall have to leave it to you clever people to sort it out.'

It was getting late and Geoff thanked Lesley for coming and helping them with their thinking. The group was just going to break up when, to everyone's surprise, Janice spoke. 'I've been listening to what you all have been saying,' she said, 'and I found it very interesting. But there is something that I would like to talk to you about. Would you like to come round to my place next week so that I can tell you about it?' Intrigued, they agreed a time.

Questions for discussion

1. Lesley pointed out that people in the Old Testament didn't believe in life after death, and yet worshipped God. How far do you think that belief in a future life is an essential part of religious faith?

2. Allison thought that people at the time of Jesus were as confused about what happens after death as we are. How do you think we should interpret the sayings of Jesus that the friends quoted? How do you react to the beliefs of Mary's Catholic colleague?

3. How does the computer program analogy strike you?

4. There seems a lot of confusion in the ideas about what happens after death in this chapter. What do you think happens?

8

A Near-Death Experience

It was only the original group of friends that met in Janice's home. Allison had phoned to say that unfortunately she couldn't come, and Lesley was tied up in her college. After they had been supplied with tea, coffee, and home-made cakes, Janice said, 'As you know, I don't really like talking about religion in public. I regard my faith as a very personal thing. But something has happened that puzzles me and I would like to know what you think about it. It's a long story.'

She went back to one night some time ago. Her neighbour, Monica, had woken her up at three o'clock in great distress. Rupert had been getting odd turns from time to time, but he had refused to pay any attention to them. Now it seemed he'd had a heart attack. Monica had phoned 999 for an ambulance, but asked Janice if she would come and sit with her while they waited. Of course, she had dressed quickly and gone round.

She found Rupert rather worse than she had expected, and suddenly he stopped breathing. Neither Monica nor Janice had any first aid experience, but remembering what they had seen on TV they were just trying mouth to mouth resuscitation when the bell rang and the paramedics were there. Efficiently they took Rupert to the ambulance and soon his heart was beating again and he was breathing.

It was a fortnight before they let him come home. Although they had been neighbours for almost ten years and were quite friendly, they had never been ones constantly to pop into each other's houses, but Rupert's heart attack had changed that, and Janice found herself almost as much at home in Monica's house as in her own.

One day when Monica was out Rupert saw her in her garden and invited her to come and join him for a cup of tea. It was a beautiful afternoon, and, as they watched the birds bathing in the pond and felt the peace of the garden that Monica worked

34

so hard in, Rupert had become thoughtful and began to tell her about his experience that dreadful night six months before.

'It was a strange thing,' he said. 'I didn't feel at all afraid. No pain. No anxiety. I suppose you'd call it an overwhelming sense of peace. I've never felt so quietly happy. Much more than now, pleasant though it is in the garden. I just can't describe it. It was wonderful.

'I seemed to float out of my body and hang over it. I could see you and Monica frantically pressing the chest of a man on the bed and blowing into his mouth, but it didn't affect me. I was just curious about what you were trying to do. Whether you succeeded in what you were doing didn't seem to matter to me at all.

'After hovering there for quite a long time I started to float into a dark tunnel. Soon I was rushing along very fast. It wasn't like running at all. I didn't have to make any effort. I wasn't in the least afraid of the dark. I could see a pinpoint of light at the end of the tunnel, which grew larger and larger very quickly. The light was golden – brilliant, and "warm" in a funny sort of way. Well, not really "warm" like this sunshine. Quite different. I can't describe it. All I know is that I longed just to stay there.

'Suddenly I came to a barrier between me and the light, and I knew that I couldn't go beyond it. It was like a gate. I pushed, but it wouldn't move. I realized that it wasn't my time to go. I knew that Monica still needed me and I must go back. I'm not sure whether I chose to return or whether I was being "sent back". All I know is that at that moment I woke up and found myself back in my body, and not feeling very comfortable at all in that hospital bed.

'I often think about it. Once you've had an experience like that it's something that you can't forget. It was too vivid. And just too marvellous.'

Janice told them that Rupert's voice had become rather dreamy, but now he gave a little start and looked across at her with a rather shamefaced grin. 'It must sound very weird to you,' he said. Janice assured him that she didn't find it weird at all. It was extremely interesting.

'As you all know,' she said, 'I never like asking people about their religious feelings, but sitting there in the garden it seemed the natural thing to do. "Can I ask you a personal question?" I said. "You had this wonderful experience of life after death and yet you don't come to church. Hasn't it made any difference to your belief about God?"'

'Not at all,' he said, brightly. 'I didn't find anything "religious" about that experience – not at all. Oh, I know some people who have had experiences like mine say that they have met Jesus, or Mary, or whatever saint or God they believe in. But I didn't meet anyone at all. Some people say they talked to relatives who had died. I didn't. All I had was just a feeling of peace in that golden light.'

Janice told them that she asked whether it had made any difference to him at all. 'Oh yes,' Rupert replied, 'it's made a lot of difference. I've lost all fear of death. When it finally comes I now know that it will be pleasant and not something dreadful. All the aches and pains we suffer in our bodies will go away completely. Death is something almost to look forward to. I don't think I've changed in any other way. Perhaps I've become a bit more sympathetic to other people's problems. Not that I feel I want to talk about my experience. You're the first person I've told all this. But I do try to cheer people up if they're depressed.' He laughed. 'No,' he said, 'you're not going to convert me. I'm too old for that.' Janice told them that she had laughed too. She certainly had no intention of trying to convert anyone.

Janice told her friends that she kept on turning what Rupert had said over and over in her mind the whole of that evening, and she hadn't been able to put it out of her mind since. She found it strange that he hadn't become religious after he had almost died – perhaps had actually been 'dead' for a few minutes. His experience seemed to have very little to do with religion. All he seemed certain about was that death was nothing to be feared and that he would continue to exist in some kind of glorious after-life. Was it like that with everyone who had had a near-death experience? she wondered.

The friends were silent for quite a long time. Janice had told the story so vividly that they almost travelled with Rupert through that tunnel. It was Mary who spoke first.

'You'll all think I'm an awful sceptic,' she said, 'but the explanation seems quite straightforward to me. George hadn't really died. Not absolutely. Dying takes a long time, and the various parts of the body 'die' at different paces. His experiences were just as 'physical' as our feelings now. Perhaps it was a drop in his blood pressure, or loss of oxygen reaching the brain, which produced those hallucinations. I don't believe it offers any evidence for what happens after death at all.'

She looked round the group, expecting violent reactions to what she had just said. Instead everyone obviously wanted to tread carefully. Fred spoke first. 'You'll be surprised at this,' he said, 'but I'm inclined to agree with Mary. I don't like all this interest in ghosts and spiritualism and the occult today. It's unhealthy as well as being unchristian. I don't think we ought to meddle with such things. And I certainly don't think that strange experiences like those Janice has told us about provide any evidence for life after death. It's a matter of faith in Jesus.'

Alec was even more hostile. 'I agree with Fred,' he said, 'but I'd go even further. What Rupert experienced bears no relation to the Christian belief in judgment, heaven and hell. It suggests that everyone goes to a cosy heaven when they die, and I can't accept that at all.'

Geoff looked at Anne, who seemed worried. 'I don't know what to think,' she said. 'I'm inclined to go along with Mary, but I'm not sure. You see, if Rupert had experienced things that he'd expected, I'd be inclined to agree that it was a hallucination produced by his physical condition. But it was obviously quite unexpected. He didn't meet God, or Jesus, or any members of his family who had died. I'd be much more sceptical if a Christian told me she had met Jesus, and described him like one of the paintings, or if a Catholic had said he had seen the Virgin Mary and she was exactly like the statue in his church. But this seems different. And I'm impressed by the fact that it *didn't* make Rupert religious. It all seems authentic somehow.' She paused, and then added, 'I wonder what was beyond the barrier.'

Alec repeated his objections to treating Rupert's experience seriously as a proof that there was a life after death, but Fred reminded him of St Paul. 'He had an experience of being caught up into the third heaven. He heard things in Paradise which he tells us it isn't lawful for any human being to utter. Perhaps he had the same kind of experience as Rupert had. Remember that Paul uses strange language. "I know a man in Christ, fourteen years ago (whether in the body, I know not; or whether out of the body, I know not; God knows)." It is so like Rupert, who said he looked down on his body but didn't know who it was. And Paul doesn't say that it was Jesus who spoke to him, though he was quite certain that the risen Christ met him on the Damascus road. He just heard words.'

Again everyone was silent. This was obviously something they couldn't take in quickly, although Alec remained firm in his opinion. At last Geoff spoke. 'Perhaps we need to go away and think about it,' he said. But Anne interrupted. 'Geoff, it's not fair. We've all said what we think, but you haven't told us what your reaction is.' Curiously, Geoff seemed nonplussed. 'This is really out of my orbit,' he said at last. 'I'm quite clear about how to approach the Bible. As you all know, I take a very relaxed attitude. And I'm pretty clear about the problem of suffering. But when it comes to the paranormal I'm not sure. I know some people try to treat it scientifically, but from what little I've read, it seems to me that you can't apply the kind of tests that scientists expect. Oh, I know that there have been experiments with telepathy, but it seems to me that the results have been inconclusive. And what has telepathy to do with the kind of experiences that Rupert had? I would like to agree with Mary, but there are still little niggles in my mind.' He laughed. 'You'll all say I'm getting too old for this kind of exploration!' He turned to Janice. 'I'm sure we all want to thank you for a most interesting evening, even if it has left some of us more confused than before.'

Questions for discussion

1. Do you know anyone who has had a near-death experience? If so, what was their experience like? In what ways did it differ from Rupert's?

2. Rupert didn't regard his near-death experience as in any way 'religious'. Do you find this surprising? Why? (or why not?)

3. Discuss the responses of each of the friends to Rupert's experience. What do you think about it? (Fred's reference to Paul is II Corinthians 12.1–5.)

9

Archie's 'Funeral'

Everyone knew Mrs Marsh. Each day, morning and evening, and often in the afternoon, without fail, rain or shine, snow or gale, she was out walking her toy poodle, Archie. You never saw her without him by her side. He was the only real companion she had now that her husband had died. Before that they had both taken their dog out for walks in all weathers. He was a lively little chap, always bouncy and bright – and obedient too, unlike many dogs that you used to meet when you were out walking.

Then Archie died. Mrs Marsh was devastated. She would have liked to have him buried in the churchyard, but she realized that this wouldn't be possible. So she arranged a funeral in her garden. Although it was a struggle, she dug his grave herself and invited her neighbours and a few friends, including Mary, Anne, Fred and Geoff. When Fred heard that there was to be a burial service he felt he couldn't come. Alec was more dismissive. 'Who ever heard of a funeral for a dog?' he declared. Mrs Marsh had asked the vicar to say prayers, but he too said that he really didn't think he could take a service in this official way.

Anne wondered what kind of a service it would be. She discovered that Mrs Marsh had made up some prayers, thanking God for Archie's life and for the happiness that he had given her, and praying that God would take care of him. She had put him in a strong cardboard box, on his favourite blanket and put some dog biscuits in with him. She solemnly lowered this into the grave and said the words from the burial service: 'Forasmuch as it has pleased Almighty God of his great mercy to take unto himself the soul of dear Archie: we therefore commit his body to the ground; earth to earth, ashes to ashes, dust to dust' and even added 'in sure and certain hope of the resurrection'. Anne was glad Fred and Alec hadn't come, and that many of those who crowded round the grave that Mrs Marsh had dug weren't churchgoers. Afterwards Mrs Marsh brought out cups of tea and glasses of sherry, and pieces of a cake that she had baked specially.

Anne, Mary and Geoff walked back home silent with their own thoughts. They reached Mary's house first and on an impulse she invited them in. 'I just must have someone to talk to,' she said.

No one knew how to begin, and rather lamely Mary said, 'Well, what do you think about that?'

Anne said she was puzzled. What came into her mind as she stood by Archie's grave – and she was very diffident about saying it – was that Archie was in fact more of a friend to Mrs Marsh than a baby that had died when only a day old could possibly be to its parents. Why, then, did we all assume that the baby went to heaven while the dog was just dead?

'What a weird thing to say!' said Mary, but Geoff pressed Anne a bit more. 'Why did you think that?', he asked. Anne wasn't sure. She supposed it was because Mrs Marsh had built up a relationship with Archie, while it is only gradually that a baby becomes a real person and a member of the family.

'Do you mean,' said Mary, remembering what they had said on that seat in the cemetery after they had looked at those rows of children's graves, 'that you think that somehow a dog like Archie is more of a "person" than the baby, and so there is more of a "something" to go on living after death?'

'Put like that it seems stupid,' Anne admitted, but Geoff butted in with, 'No, not stupid. I think you may have a point.' But Anne did feel that she had been silly, and added that she supposed that one of the things that made human beings different from animals was that they had been made in the image of God. It was because they were in God's image that they might go to heaven when animals were dead and done for.

'Hold on,' Geoff said. 'What do you mean by trotting out that phrase, "made in the image of God"?' Anne thought for some moments. She had just said it without really thinking. It was what everyone said. You heard parsons defending caring for the poor on the grounds that everyone was made in God's image. When she confessed all this, Geoff gave one of his smiles, at once so reassuring and so irritating. 'That's what I thought,' he said. 'So the modern woman, who had all that trouble over some bits of the Bible and accepts the evolution of all life on earth, still goes back for refuge to the beginning of Genesis.'

Anne laughed. It was just like Geoff – and how right he was. But then, how were human beings different from other animals? She was faced with a dilemma. If human beings who had evolved from the earlier forms of animate life had some kind of life after death, why shouldn't animals? But if human beings really were different from animals, she was back with the problem that they had mentioned before: at what point in their evolution did the hominids obtain souls – or at what point did God decide to raise them from the dead?

She knew that Alec would have had no doubts. To him, animals were just part of the natural world which was a stage for the drama of the 'salvation of man', as he would have put it. Salvation depended on faith in Jesus. It was his death on the cross which saved us from our sins – but only human beings. She knew that he could never understand why people made so much fuss about vivisection and experiments on animals. In the end a dog was no different from a slug or an ant, and it was just being sentimental to suppose anything else. He had no time for all this fuss about lambs gambolling in the fields. It was sad for Mrs Marsh, but she would simply have to get another dog.

Mary had stayed very quiet. Now she put in: 'I can't stop thinking about Mrs Marsh. She is more lonely now even than when her husband died, because she has no one left at all. Archie meant a very great deal to her. If people look for life after death mainly because they think they will be reunited with their loved ones, won't heaven be less than heaven to Mrs Marsh if Archie isn't there? Oh, I know I'm all mixed up, but I don't think we can leave animals out of this. Whatever you may say, a dog is part of the family.'

Geoff felt that he had been unfeeling. Both Mary and Anne were upset. 'I'm sorry,' he said. 'Can we look at this again? As I see it, two important things come out of Archie's burial. We have to think again about whether human beings are different from animals in such a way that they have a life after death – or at least some of them do – while animals don't. And that's not easy to decide, because we all accept that we are all part of the chain of evolution. Anne's question whether some animals are more of a person than a new-born baby is the other thing that is worth thinking about. We've got to be careful here. Allison told me once that, as a chaplain at the hospital, she is often asked to take the funerals of still-born babies and those who have died within a few hours of their birth. She has watched their parents holding the dead baby and knows that they think of it as a person. Sometimes she has been asked to baptize such babies. She explained to me that most chaplains would not think that it is appropriate to baptize babies who have died, but she was often torn between what seemed right theologically and what she felt as a woman standing beside the grieving parents. So I'm almost afraid to say anything.

'I suppose we would agree that although we are born with our own genetic makeup, the personality we develop largely depends upon our contacts with other people – our parents, our brothers and sisters, if we have any, and all the other people we meet. But then, are we thinking about animals in terms that are too human, when we talk about a dog's faithfulness or obedience? Isn't it just following its natural instincts? We like to think that our dog is a member of the family, but the dog just thinks that he is a member of the pack, and we are the pack leaders. Oh yes, and we ought to ask why the vicar refused to say a prayer at Archie's "funeral".'

'It's all getting too complicated for me', said Mary. I don't know the answers to any of your questions. Anne wanted to push Geoff a bit more. 'Over the last few weeks,' she said, 'we seem to have done a demolition job on pretty well every possible belief in life after death. Do you really think that we are really just like animals and that death is the end?'

Geoff suddenly became serious. 'I don't know,' he said, 'and I find that very difficult to live with. I thought that I had worked out a pretty satisfactory philosophy of life. I read the Bible for pleasure and get great inspiration from many parts of it, but I don't worry myself about its "authority". I think that is the wrong way to look at it. I'm not very sure what people mean when they talk about providence, but I don't find that it makes my life any less happy, or means that I feel any less secure. I'm certain of God, but I don't expect him to bale me out when I get into a fix. I suppose Alec would call me a "deist". I'm prepared to admit that there are many things I don't understand or I'm not sure about. But with life after death it's another matter. I keep on thinking of when my father died. I looked down at him in his coffin and into my mind the unwanted words came, "For all I know, that's the end of you, Dad." And I was angry. Because I knew that I cared. Whether there was a life after death mattered more to me at that moment than anything else. It is still the most important thing in the world.'

'So you don't put yourself with those people who say they are Christians and come to church regularly and yet say that it doesn't matter whether they survive death or not, and the important thing is to worship God and live a good life here and now, and help other people as much as you can?' said Anne.

'No,' Geoff replied.

They were all very quiet. Mary thought of her own father and mother. Anne remembered those children's graves.

'Ah well,' Geoff said at last, 'I suppose we shall never know. As one Christian scientist said, there is only one experiment which will test our hypothesis. It's called dying.'

Questions for discussion

1. What is your reaction to the funeral Mrs Marsh arranged for Archie? Why do you think like that?

2. Why do you think the vicar refused to say a prayer at Archie's 'funeral'?

3. How would you distinguish between Archie and a baby who died at less than a week old?

Part 2

Thinking Through the Issues

10

What is Being Offered for Belief?

The discussions among the group of friends have shown up the main difficulty in trying to confirm a belief in life after death: there are so many different ideas that it is far from easy to discover what is being offered for belief. It is not just a matter of the difficulty of believing, or of examining the arguments and determining which are valid. Rather it is necessary to ask whether we are being asked to believe in 'immortality of the soul' or 'resurrection of the body', or something else, and what each of these might mean. Even in the Bible there seems to be no clear-cut belief, although, as we shall see, the church attempted to develop one, and the drama of creation, the Fall, salvation, heaven and hell has dominated much of the Christian era. So we shall begin by collecting up the main points that arise from the discussions in the first part of this book.

Mary found it difficult to know what remained of a person that could continue to exist after the individual had died. Her father had believed that his wife would be restored to the young girl he had known and loved before she had succumbed to Alzheimer's disease. He was confident that she was 'with Jesus' and that when he died, they would be reunited. But to Mary the disease had destroyed her mother's personality, so that there was nothing to survive. And even though it was somewhat easier to think of her father as continuing to exist, since he had died with his mental powers unimpaired, she could not see *what* could still live. The 'person' seemed to be linked so closely with the body, and especially with the brain, that the death of the body seemed to involve total extinction (chapters 1 and 2).

Anne and Mary followed up some of these doubts. Life goes on for those who are 'left'. They change. Their relationships with other people alter. But if we assume that those who die

49

remain as they were at the point of death, what will those who die many years later have in common with them? (chapter 4).

Geoff emphasized that a large part of the difficulty in accepting life after death is a failure of the imagination. We only know life on earth, life in our physical world. How can we possibly imagine what life might be like in a purely 'spiritual' existence? (chapters 2 and 5).

What is involved in 'immortality' and 'resurrection' ran through much of the discussion, and we shall need to look closely at these concepts. Some difficulties about both were brought out during the discussions between the friends. Is immortality of the soul properly a 'Christian' idea, since the Bible mostly works with 'resurrection'? But does the idea of resurrection mean that God creates a 'replica' or a 'clone'? Immortality involves believing in a spiritual 'soul', but how are we to relate this soul to the body – and how does evolution affect the belief? Does it help to think of the 'soul' as a kind of computer program? And what about the suggestion that we shall continue to 'exist' in God's memory? (chapters 5 and 7).

Ideas of heaven and hell raised other kinds of questions. Would it be moral for God to consign sinners to everlasting punishment? Can we escape the problem by holding that God's justice is different from ours and we shall only arrive at full understanding in the afterlife? And underlying the whole discussion is Mary's doubt about whether anything exists after death to be assigned to heaven or hell (chapter 6).

Running though many of the discussions is the place of biblical teaching. Fred and Alec, in their different ways, fastened on this. Lesley pointed out how inconclusive this evidence is and earlier Allison had stressed that Jesus was a man of his own age. Linked with this is the relation of the resurrection of Jesus to life after death for his followers (chapters 3, 6, 7). We shall need to look carefully at the biblical evidence.

Mary mentioned Christian tradition, especially the Catholic belief in purgatory (chapter 7). Protestants tend to undervalue the place of tradition, but it cannot be neglected if we are to arrive at a rounded Christian understanding.

Chapter 8 recounted a Near-Death experience, compiled from a number of such accounts recorded by several researchers. How are such experiences to be explained?

The death of a pet raised several issues, besides the question of whether life after death is limited to human beings. How far will a greatly loved pet be needed to complete the happiness of heaven for its owner? To what extent is interaction with other human beings part of what it means to be 'human' and to have a 'personality'? (chapter 9).

A point which did not come out clearly in the discussions between the friends but which has to be taken into account is the relation between philosophical arguments and Christian tradition (including the teaching of the Bible). Many of the arguments which were put forward by the friends were philosophical rather than Christian in a narrow sense. Does this mean that they rest upon presuppositions which may not be Christian in a traditional sense? If so, what weight should the Christian place on them?

The first thing we need to do, therefore, is to sort out the different ideas, so that we know what it is that is being offered for belief.

To do

No questions are attached to this chapter because it looks back on the previous discussions. Readers may find it useful, however, before they go on to the rest of the book to re-read chapters 1–9 in the light of the list of issues set out here.

11

The Immortal Soul

We have seen how vague and confused ideas about life after death usually are. It will be useful, therefore, to start by trying to clarify our minds about some terms that are frequently used in discussion of the subject. We begin with the soul.

It has been common until very recently to speak of 'body and soul' as the two components of the human individual. These ideas go back a very long way in European thought, but it was Plato who gave the main impetus to the idea of an immortal soul, and it is Descartes who has been condemned by many modern thinkers for positing 'the ghost in the machine'. We shall concentrate on these two philosophers.

In popular Greek thought the soul was conceived as a kind of breath or vapour which animated the body and at death continued a weak, shadowy existence. Even though it did not 'die' absolutely, the future life was certainly not a happy or desirable one. In Homer the souls cannot speak to Odysseus until they have drunk the blood of the living to give them strength. We shall see that these ideas are closely similar to those of the Old Testament (chapter 13). The question of whether the future life is desirable or not is important.

Plato, who was strongly influenced by Pythagoreanism and Orphic religion, had a much richer idea. He thought of the soul as the inner self, the true person. It was immortal in the full sense that it had neither beginning nor end. Imprisoned in the body, its fulfilment lay in being purified and ascending to the realm of eternal goodness, and this was the aim of philosophy. Thus he taught a strong dualism between soul and body, to the denigration of the body.[1]

---

[1] How far these are the ideas of Socrates is uncertain. In Plato's dialogues Socrates is the speaker, but certainly in the later ones it is Plato's own ideas that are presented. Here I use Plato throughout.

He argued that the lover of wisdom will seek to nurture his soul through education and training. Indeed, 'true philosophers make dying their profession', since their occupation consists in 'the freeing and separation of soul from body'. Among his arguments for the immortality of the soul three are the most widely known, although none is convincing. The first is the argument from recollection. Plato holds that before it entered into its present relation with the body, the soul possessed all knowledge. True knowledge, therefore, consists of recollecting the truths that the soul already knows, and in the *Meno* he performs an experiment on a slave boy by asking him leading questions about a mathematical problem to elicit 'knowledge' which, unwittingly, the boy already possessed. Strictly, of course, even if this were valid, it would only prove the pre-existence of the soul and not its immortality. But in fact Plato has been teaching the boy through his questions.

His second argument is even less convincing. He claims that opposites are produced from opposites, e.g., waking from sleeping, and so there is a cycle of life–death–life. This rests on the unproved assumption of an eternal cyclic process and the equally unproved belief that opposites are produced by opposites.

The third argument depends on his overall philosophical view that the present world is a 'copy' of the real world of the 'forms' – a kind of eternal, spiritual world. He declares that the soul is akin to the forms, and like them is immortal. Even on his own theory, however, this is hardly cogent, since the forms are changeless and exist outside of time, and strictly there would be a form of 'soul' as well as of all the other features in the natural world.

All this, even if accepted, would prove no more than that the soul was long-lived, as Cebes in the *Phaedo* points out. It might eventually 'wear out'. To this Plato has no answer.

Plato made no attempt to describe what life after death is like. Instead he told a number of 'myths', but stated that 'no reasonable man ought to insist that the facts are exactly as I have described them', though he did hold that something very like them is a true account of our souls and their future habitation. He believed that the myths could inspire us with confidence about a future beyond death.

These are the ideas in the early dialogues. Plato's later thought moves away from individual immortality towards an emphasis upon the world soul into which human souls are absorbed at death. The aim of the philosopher is to lose himself in the world soul.

I have spent so long on Plato because his idea of the soul has had enormous influence on Western thought, not least within the church. Descartes can be treated more briefly.

Descartes is perhaps best-known for his aphorism: 'I think, therefore I exist.' It is in fact central to his philosophy. Determined to discover incontestable truth, he decided to reject 'everything in which I could suppose the slightest reason for doubt'. But the very fact of thinking and doubting, he maintained, meant that the 'I' who is doing the thinking must exist. From this he drew the conclusion that the essential being, the real 'I', consists of the soul, distinct from the body. This thinking soul controls the body, which is no more than a machine. (He denied that animals possess reason or soul, and therefore argued that they are simply machines.) Descartes's arguments for the existence of the soul have also been challenged, notably by Gilbert Ryle and Antony Flew. On the other hand, some leading scholars, such as H. D. Lewis, Richard Swinburne and Paul Badham, continue to accept the existence of the soul.

It would be beyond the scope of this book to examine the arguments in detail, but since some of these criticisms have filtered down into the common assumptions of men and women today, it is worth looking at them briefly. The opponents of Descartes argue that when we speak of a 'person' we mean the being that we can see, touch, hear, and talk to. We can only communicate with other people by means of our bodies. We ought not, therefore, to speak of a 'soul' as if it were a person, for it does not possess the physical features that are an essential part of what being a person means. We cannot see, touch, hear, or talk to a 'soul'. Discarding for the moment the possibility of telepathy, there is no way in which souls could relate to each other.

To this is usually added the argument that the mind is identical with the brain. Mary found it difficult to believe that any of her mother's personality remained to continue to exist after death after she had succumbed to Alzheimer's disease (chapters 1 and 2). Descartes was aware of the difficulty. He realized that his arguments showed only that it is logically possible to distinguish between mind and brain. He accepted that in practice it is impossible to prove that it is not the brain which is thinking rather than the soul, but he nevertheless retained his dualism of body and soul. Modern medical research into the brain has often been taken to support the view that the mind is nothing other than the brain. In the same way, memory, which might be regarded as an activity of the soul and without which it is difficult to think of continued personal identity, seems to be dependent on our brain cells.

Another objection to the theory is that it is too individualistic. As Geoff pointed out (chapter 9), although we each have our own genetic makeup, our personality develops through interaction with other people. While it is not impossible to present a version of the theory of the soul in which such development is possible, in itself the theory seems to mean that each soul is formed complete and fully developed and simply has to be joined (Ryle mockingly called it 'harnessed', as if it were a physical or material object) to the body. And in any case any development of the soul would have to be worked out by means of the body. This might suggest that the soul was in some way 'imperfect' and needed the body.

These are serious objections and it is not satisfactory to push them aside as 'reductionist', that is, as reducing human personality to the physical and material body, so that the mind is no more than the brain.

Those who defend the existence of the soul argue in reply that when we look at ourselves inwardly we are very reluctant to accept that there is no 'me' beyond my physical body and brain. It is 'I' who have toothache. To speak simply of the stimulation of some brain cells seems totally inadequate.

Moreover, the difficulty of the stroke victim or the sufferer from Alzheimer's disease can be met by pointing out that belief in the soul does not imply that the soul communicates directly with the world outside the body. If the brain is the agent through which the soul acts, then damage to the brain will impair the ability of the soul to act and communicate, even to think, but this should be understood as a 'blockage' rather than as a partial destruction of the person. Persons who have had strokes tell of the frustration they experienced in not being able to communicate ideas that were quite clear in their own minds.

Today many Christians thinkers have abandoned the idea of the soul, partly because they find the arguments against it persuasive, partly because they regard belief in the resurrection as the truly 'Christian' belief . We shall come back to this later.

Questions for discussion

1. What picture of the soul do you have?

2. Which among the arguments for and against the existence of the soul do you find most convincing? Are there any other arguments that you would like to put forward?

3. What part do you think philosophical arguments such as those presented in this chapter have to play in Christian belief?

12

Resurrection of the Body

Many thinkers today reject the idea of an immortal soul for the reasons given in the last chapter. Some think that our personality is so closely related to the physical body that death is the end. Others adopt some form of resurrection belief. To this we now turn.

There are several reasons for this renewed interest in the idea of resurrection. The most important is probably that such a belief accepts the unity of the human person. This avoids the problems with the idea of a soul within the body that were mentioned in the last chapter. It is also thought to fit in more easily with modern medical and psychological theory. Some Christians are attracted to it on the grounds that it is biblical, whereas they regard the idea of an immortal soul as coming from Greek thought and therefore as being 'pagan'.

As we shall see in the next chapter, the idea of an individual resurrection arrived late in Israelite thought, and then it took several different forms.

A literal bringing of dead bodies back to life can be pushed aside. It is almost impossible to conceive. How could all the particles that made up the body of the person who has died be collected together again and formed into a living body? Some, if not all, of them will have been combined into other bodies and natural objects. Moreover, such a resurrected body would be subject to ageing and death and so any future life would only be for a short time. It also implies the continuation of life in a physical world akin to our own planet.

Paul was aware of this difficulty. He spoke of a 'spiritual body' (see I Corinthians 15.35–50). There is no inherent difficulty with this idea, although again it is difficult to imagine what such a spiritual body might be like. It has been described in an official Church of England doctrinal statement as 'an appropriate organ of expression and activity'. These terms are

57

so abstract that they tell us little. But certainly the only tenable theory of resurrection must accept that the resurrected body will be different from the earthly body.

Any resurrection hope involves at least two things. First, it accepts that those who have died are really 'dead'. Life is extinct. Nothing survives. Thus the resurrection is a miracle performed by God. It can almost be described as a new creation. Second, if it is to be a genuine 'resurrection' of the person who has died, there must be some continuity between the dead person and the resurrected one. In particular there must be a persistence of memory and character.

The first presents no problems, since it is clearly within divine possibility. God is able to do anything apart from what is logically impossible (he cannot make $2 + 2$ equal 5 or create a stone too heavy for him to lift!), and there is no inherent impossibility in the recreation of dead persons into a different sphere of life.

The second is more difficult. It will be recalled that Geoff wondered whether the resurrected person would be no more than a replica or clone (chapter 5). Perhaps we should distinguish between the two. A replica has no direct links with the original apart from looking the same, perhaps even being the same in every detail. It is, however, not *the same* as the original. In a clone some physical matter from the original is carried across and controls its development. And if anything is carried over after death we are back with some form of 'soul' theory. If the individual is made up of a single 'person', seen in his or her body, then what is carried over must be part of that body – an immortal part, if that is not a contradiction.

Sometimes the resurrection body has been thought of as a transformed body (and as we shall see in chapter 15, the resurrection of Jesus has been interpreted by one scholar as involving such a transformation, but he suggests that this happened three days after his death and before his body had decayed into its elements). It is exceedingly difficult to see what this can mean, and few of those who espouse the theory feel sufficiently bold to spell it out. Given modern physics and the understanding of matter as a form of energy, it is not a total impossibility. What would be offered for belief would be some kind of rarefied body, sufficiently similar to the body of flesh and blood for memory to be carried over and for it to be recognized by other equally rarefied bodies. Some would say we are approaching science fiction. We must conclude that no currently available resurrection theory solves the problem of continuity, especially if we link memory closely with the brain. This is perhaps the most serious weakness of the resurrection belief. How can it be overcome?

John Hick has presented a most elaborate account of 'the resurrection of the person'. He accepts that the only self that we know is the 'walking, talking, acting, sleeping individual who lives, it may be, for some sixty or eighty years and then dies'. There is no room in this view for a soul, and certainly no possibility of a soul which survives the death of the body. After death, however, God, by an act of sovereign power, 'resurrects or reconstitutes or recreates him', not as the identical physical human being that he was before death, but as a 'spiritual body'. To maintain continuity with the deceased, Hick holds that this resurrected person possesses the same character and memory as the person who had died. What has been created is an *exact* replica of the deceased, but in a different 'space'.

This still leaves the difficulty of how this replica can be the *same* person as the one who had died. Hick meets this by stressing the exact similarity between the two. The replica possesses the 'memory, emotions and volition' of the original. More precisely, the 'stream of consciousness' of the deceased continues in the replica at the point where it left off when he died. In this case, he argues, it is perverse to deny that it is the same person as the one he remembers himself to be.

There are two things to be said about this intriguing hypothesis. The first is that it is difficult to see how the

59

spiritual replica can possess precisely the 'memory, emotions and volition' of the original, since it is now existing in a different 'space'. All the aspects of our thinking relate to the physical world, to our life on planet earth. How can they be the same in a spiritual world? The second derives from the first. Even if the fact of the identical replica existing in a different space is accepted, and even though the replica supposes himself to be the deceased, this is only what the replica supposes. It is not 'wantonly paradoxical', as Hick claims, to rule that the replica is not the same person. In effect, of course, it does not matter, since for the replica it is as if he continues to exist. Perhaps this is sufficient for faith.

Some theologians retain their doubts. A suggestion offered by one of them will occupy us in the next chapter.

Questions for discussion

1. What do you consider to be the strengths of a resurrection faith?

2. What is your reaction to Hick's presentation of the exact replica of the person who has died?

3. How do you think each of the friends would react to Hick's proposal?

13

In the Memory of God

Professor John Macquarrie finds himself unable to accept either the idea of an immortal soul or the doctrine of the resurrection of the body. Not that he wishes to dismiss either out of hand. But he thinks that most of the speculations about the nature of the resurrection body are 'so ingenious and far-fetched as to strain credibility to the uttermost'. John Hick's proposal of an exact replica in a different 'space' he regards as bizarre. Many will no doubt react to his own suggestion in a similar way.

He sees the self as 'a pattern in time', just as the body is 'a pattern disposed in space'. The soul is inseparable from the body, but is distinct in that it is to be understood in terms of time, while the body is to be viewed in terms of space. Neither is dependent upon the other. Certainly, he rejects a materialism which sees the soul as a kind of projection by the body. One feature of human beings is their ability to move beyond a succession of momentary experiences and hold past, present and future together. We are able to look back to the past and look forward to the future, while living in the present.

In the same way we may suppose that God gathers up all time. If this is so then, Macquarrie claims, our destiny is not to live on as immortal souls, but to be gathered up in the experience of God.

The main question to be asked of this proposal is whether it offers any real continuing existence for the individual. Jacques Pohier, a Dominican priest, was forbidden by the Vatican to preach, preside at the eucharist, and teach theology because one of his books was regarded as heretical. In a later book he declared that he remained a Christian but no longer believed that human beings survive death. What he had now come to believe was that when he died he would give his life back to God. He does not possess an immortal soul, and will not be raised up to a new and everlasting life through a resurrection.

Others will remember him for a time. God will remember him to all eternity. Is Macquarrie's view just this?

Macquarrie denies it. 'I have in mind a much more lively and realistic relation than simply memory. I do not mean that we shall remain fixed and unchanged for ever in God's memory. ... I mean something much more dynamic, namely, being taken up and participating in the life of God himself.' He even believes that God can transform his past life, not in the sense that he can alter what has happened, but through healing and transforming the experiences he can make them appear different. As an analogy he points out that we often view past events in our lives in a different way as we grow older. A bitter disappointment may have turned out to have been for our good. Hardship or sorrow are seen to have made us better persons. This possibility of transformation, he holds, is part of the meaning of the Cross. He also believes that such a conception fits in with modern scientific ideas of time and space that have been opened up by the theories of Einstein.

In the end, however, he bases his hope in simple trust. His belief 'rests finally on this, that if God is indeed the God of love revealed in Jesus Christ, then death will not wipe out his care for the persons he has created'. We are reminded of Ron.

What are we to say about this? Certainly simply to identify the future life of an individual as God's memory of him or her is less than the traditional Christian hope, and would not seem to represent what anyone would regard as life after death. Macquarrie accepts this. It is possible, nevertheless, that we shall have to go along with Pohier and accept that this is all that the form of our existence within a chain of birth and death over the long years of evolution permits. What Macquarrie claims, however, is that his theory goes beyond a mere memory to a living memory in which the individual continues to 'exist' in some real sense. Perhaps the doubt we have about this is whether it is an intelligible idea.

Questions for discussion

1. How do you react to the suggestion that our only future is to be a memory in the mind of God?

2. Consider whether Macquarrie has managed to present an intelligible hypothesis.

3. Pohier claimed, 'Once I had stopped attaching value to the realities of the life of faith by believing that they lasted for ever, I discovered more of their value and their depth here and now.' What value and truth do you find in this claim?

14

Life and Death in the Old Testament

We turn from such speculations to the Bible, and first trace ideas of life and death in the Old Testament and the Jewish writings that are usually referred to as the inter-testamental literature.

Before addressing a number of texts which seem to point to a belief in life after death, we shall consider the general background beliefs of the ancient Israelites.

The Israelites did not think of human beings as having a body and soul; rather they saw the individual as being a unit of vital force, depending on the breath of God for life. A good example of this is Genesis 2.7, where God breathes into the little clay man that he has made and the creature '*becomes* a living being'.

At death this unit of vital force is broken up. Some energy may remain for a time in the parts of the body, but the dead pass into *sheol*, a land of dust and darkness, thought of as being under the ground as a kind of massive grave. There they are weak and helpless, and cut off from God. The dead kings mock the king of Babylon when he descends into *sheol*, crying out that he has now become weak as they are (Isaiah 14.9–11). So death is effectively the end. Lesley (chapter 7) referred to the woman of Tekoa, who said to David, 'We must all die, we are like water spilt on the ground, which cannot be gathered up again.' Death, then, was regarded as entirely natural. What was desired was to enjoy a long life in health and prosperity and to die in a ripe old age, with many descendants. Job likens such a death to a 'shock of grain' which 'comes up to the threshing floor in its season' (Job 5.25–26), while a prophet looks forward to the time when everyone will live to a hundred and no infants will live but a few days (Isaiah 65.20–21). Moses is said to have died in old age and with his physical powers unabated. We are probably wrong in thinking that the story in

Genesis 3 means that human beings were originally created immortal and lost their immortality because of their disobedience. Death is a normal part of life.

To return to *sheol*. It is often referred to as 'the pit' and 'destruction'. It is a place of forgetfulness, of shades and darkness. Fellowship with God is impossible there. Certainly no happy future life is experienced there. At best it is a pale reflection of life in this world of light, where God is active. The psalms provide good examples of the way the Israelites viewed death and *sheol*. In Psalm 88 a sick man cries out to God:

> My soul is full of troubles,
>   and my life draws near to Sheol.
>   . . .
> Do you work wonders for the dead?
>   Do the shades rise up to praise you?
> Is your steadfast love declared in the grave,
>   or your faithfulness in Abaddon [destruction]?
> Are your wonders known in the darkness,
>   or your saving help in the land of forgetfulness?

It is the land of no return, as Job declares:

> As the cloud fades and vanishes,
>   So those who go down to Sheol do not come up;
> they return no more to their houses,
>   nor do their places know them any more (Job 7.9–10).

He pleads with God to give him a little comfort

> before I go, never to return
>   to the land of gloom and deep darkness,
> the land of gloom and chaos,
>   where light is like darkness (Job 10.21–22).

This is the general belief right through the Old Testament, and the very few texts which seem to look to a happy future life need to be read against this background. There are, however, a few passages that deserve to be noted.

Probably the best known is Job 19.25–27 because of the musical setting in Handel's *Messiah*: 'I know that my redeemer liveth'. Unfortunately the text in these verses is very corrupt and there is little hope of restoring it with confidence. We may well give it a Christian meaning, but we should recognize that it did not have this in the book of Job. Two things are clear. First, the word translated 'redeemer' does not carry the overtones which it has acquired in Christian tradition. It refers to the next of kin who is responsible for helping his kinsman if he has fallen into any kind of difficulty, such as debt or slavery, and will be called upon to avenge his murder. Second, the book of Job as a whole works with the *sheol* belief, as we have already seen. At most, therefore, this is a leap of faith, which is soon abandoned. But probably, it does not refer to life after death at all.

In three psalms the psalmists speak of God delivering them from *sheol*. Again, this has to be set against the general Old Testament ideas of death, and the psalmists probably mean that they trust that God will save them from *premature* death, though it is just possible that they have taken a leap of faith when they cry: 'God will ransom me from the power of Sheol, for he will receive me' (Psalm 49.15; see also 16.10; 73.24). I personally think this is unlikely.

Ezekiel's vision of the valley of dry bones (Ezekiel 37.1–10) is an allegory. As God points out to the prophet, 'these bones are the whole house of Israel'. The vision is a promise of the historical restoration of the nation.

Beliefs in a life after death for the individual appear for certain only in two very late passages. In a difficult prophecy that is preserved in Isaiah 26.18–19, there may be a hint of a resurrection of the dead in the words: 'Your dead shall live, their corpses shall rise', although some scholars think it is akin to Ezekiel's allegory and is a prophecy of a national restoration.

In fact the first, and only certain reference to an individual resurrection is Daniel 12.2:

Many of those who sleep in the dust of the earth shall awake, some to everlasting life, and some to shame and everlasting contempt.

This part of the book of Daniel almost certainly comes from about 164 BC, the time of the persecution by the Greek king Antiochus Epiphanes, when many of the Jews who were most faithful to God were being killed. Under the pressure of the death of the martyrs, it seems that a hope of a resurrection sprang up. It is not clear whether the writer of Daniel expects a general resurrection. Possibly he is simply looking for a resurrection of the martyrs so that they can receive the reward they missed during their earthly life, and of the persecutors so that they can be punished. What is important to notice is that the writer does not believe in immortality, but because he thinks of death as the end he puts forward the hope of a resurrection.

After this ideas about life and death became confused. Some Jewish writers continued to accept the *sheol* belief. There is, for example, no hint of any life after death in I Maccabees or the Wisdom of Ben Sira (Ecclesiasticus in the Apocrypha). In the New Testament the Sadducees are presented as rejecting any resurrection hope (Mark 12.18; Acts 23.8), and the Jewish historian Josephus, who took part in the Jewish rising against Rome which led to the capture of Jerusalem and the destruction of the temple in AD 70, gives a similar picture of the Sadducees, and himself held that death was final.

Ideas about the life of individuals after they have died now become linked to apocalyptic beliefs about a future 'messianic' kingdom. This kingdom is sometimes thought of as earthly, in fact a glorious reign of triumphant Jews which is not always thought of as everlasting, sometimes as a heavenly kingdom. In both there is usually the hope that those faithful Jews who have died or been killed will be raised from the dead to enjoy its joys with their fellow citizens. In II Maccabees, for example, the bodies of the righteous dead are restored, while wicked Gentiles have no resurrection. The book also contains the novel idea of making a sin-offering and praying for the dead (II Maccabees 7.14, 22–24; 12.43–45), one of the reasons why Protestants rejected the authority of the book at the Reformation. Some of the later books discuss the kind of bodies which those who are raised will have. All of these accounts hold that the dead will rise in recognizable form. In this period ideas of heaven and hell are elaborated.

Alongside these beliefs in a resurrection, however, we find ideas of immortality. In the book of Jubilees, coming probably from the second century BC, the bodies of the righteous will be raised but their bones remain in the ground. It is really a resurrection of spirits only (Jubilees 23.30–31). More often, however, it seems that Greek ideas of the immortality of the soul have been taken over. The best known of all these passages, because it has often been read in the burial service, is from the Wisdom of Solomon:

> The souls of the righteous are in the hand of God
> and no torment will ever touch them.
> In the eyes of the foolish they seemed to have died,
> and their departure was thought to be a disaster,
> and their going from us to be their destruction;
> but they are at peace.
> For though in the sight of others they were punished,
> their hope is full of immortality (Wisdom 3.1–4).

This, however, is no natural immortality. It is the souls of the *righteous* who are immortal. Immortality appears to be regarded as a reward for goodness, for the wicked pass into oblivion. A similar set of beliefs is found in IV Maccabees, where there is no hint of a resurrection. Those loyal to the law have the 'hope of salvation' and will enjoy eternal life, a life of purity, lived in God's presence. On the other hand, in this book the wicked will be punished with eternal fire and torment.

Three striking features appear from this rapid survey of Israelite and early Jewish beliefs.

First, for a very long period of history the Israelites appear to have been content to accept the finality of death. Close and joyful though fellowship with God may be, it lasts only for the extent of human life. Here is a living and exuberant religion that sees no need of a future life to round off its blessedness.

Second, it seems to have been the pressure of death of the martyrs which led to fumblings after the possibility of reward after death. For most of the Old Testament period the Israelites held that retribution was worked out in this life, despite strains which were produced by the suffering of good men and women. It was only when the supremely faithful Jews were killed in early life that this belief began to disintegrate. Some way had to be found to secure a just reward for those whose loyalty to God led to death rather than happiness.

Third, beliefs in a happy future life were indeed 'fumblings'. No single set of ideas was generally accepted, and even within individual books there were often tensions between different expectations. Confusion rather than certainty marks the early Jewish beliefs. By the time of Jesus most people probably held some expectation of a resurrection, although there were groups, such as the Sadducees, who rejected all ideas of life beyond death. The beliefs, however, were not fixed in any 'orthodox' dogma, as the New Testament itself shows, and the first Christians belonged to one extreme of a spectrum of ideas.

Questions for discussion

1. Sceptics allege that belief in life after death is wish-fulfilment. In what respects do you think the history of Israelite and early Jewish beliefs supports or contradicts this claim?

2. What difference does the fact that belief in life after death arose very late in the history of Israel make to your own faith?

3. Many Christians today argue that the true Christian faith is in resurrection rather than immortality, and point to Old Testament ideas of the nature of human life. How far do you agree with this?

15

The Resurrection of Jesus

Christian belief centres on the resurrection of Jesus and we turn to this first. Without the resurrection Jesus remains no more than one of the vast multitude of innocent sufferers that sadden the history of the human race. His life and teaching may have had greater influence on his followers and on later generations, but it remains just that – an influence. Whether the importance of his resurrection for life after death is, as the hymn says, 'Made like him, like him we rise', will have to be considered later. But without his resurrection belief in a future life will necessarily be different.

Most of us have a somewhat confused idea of the resurrection, made up of a mixture of incidents drawn from all four Gospels. Each of the Gospels, however, tells its own story, and it will be useful to sketch out these four accounts before discussing the problems that they raise for belief today.

Mark

Mark is still generally regarded as the first Gospel to be written, and almost all scholars agree that 16.9–18 is a later addition to the original work. (There is no space here to present the arguments for this conclusion beyond saying that the ten verses are missing from the best manuscripts and the style is quite different from the rest of Mark.) Whether Mark intended to end his Gospel at 16.8 or whether the last section of his Gospel was lost (or never completed) is more controversial. Since it is impossible to recover what may have been lost and to end the Gospel at 16.8 fits the spirit of the Gospel as a whole, we shall assume that Mark's final sentence was 'And they [the women] went out and fled from the tomb, for terror and amazement had seized them, and they said nothing to anyone, for they were afraid.'

71

And Mark's account of the visit of the women to the tomb fills us with terror and amazement too. For he tells of no appearances of the risen Christ. He speaks only of a tomb with the stone rolled away from the entrance, and of a young man in a white robe sitting inside the tomb who declares that Jesus has been raised, points out that the tomb is empty, and charges the women to tell the disciples 'and Peter' that Jesus is going ahead of them to Galilee where they will see him. Throughout the women are terrified.

Matthew

In striking contrast to Mark, Matthew almost describes what happened when Jesus was raised. He mentions an earthquake, and an angel who rolled back the stone, sat on it, and then talked to the women. They, quite differently from in Mark's account, run off joyfully and quickly to tell the disciples – and Jesus himself meets them as they go, and reiterates the angel's message about going to Galilee. Meanwhile the guards who, Matthew tells us earlier, had been stationed by the chief priests and Pharisees to guard the tomb against theft of the body of Jesus by his followers, had become 'like dead men' on seeing the angel. When they tell the priests, they are paid a bribe to spread the story that the disciples did in fact steal the body while they were asleep. The narrative ends with Jesus meeting the eleven remaining disciples on a mountain in Galilee, where they worshipped him, 'but some doubted'. Jesus gives them the famous mission charge to make disciples of all nations, 'baptizing them in the name of the Father and of the Son and of the Holy Spirit', telling them to keep the teaching he has given, and promising that he will be with them 'to the close of the age'.

Several features suggest that it is an account which has had many years of Christian embellishment behind it. For one thing the trinitarian baptismal formula is strange, especially as the first Christians baptized converts in the name of Jesus alone, according to the Acts of the Apostles (Acts 2.26; 8.16; 10.48).

Further, the nearest narrative to Matthew's account of the resurrection is in the 'Gospel of Peter', an anti-semitic work which almost certainly drew some of its material from the biblical Gospels but introduced some changes and additions from oral tradition. In the Gospel of Peter the members of the guard at the tomb see 'three men come out from the sepulchre, two of them supporting the other and a cross following them and the heads of the two reaching to heaven, but that of him who was being led reached beyond the heavens. And they heard a voice out of the heavens crying, "Have you preached to those who sleep?", and from the cross there was heard the answer, "Yes".' This moves far beyond anything in Matthew, and the sobriety of the biblical Gospels stands out in marked contrast to it. But it also shows that the resurrection story was embellished, and this must raise doubts about some of the features in Matthew, such as the placing of the guard.

Luke

Luke's account of the resurrection is longer than Matthew's. As well as an account of the women at the empty tomb, he records a visit to the tomb by Peter, and presents the familiar story of the journey of Cleopas and another disciple to Emmaus. On their return to Jerusalem the Eleven and their companions tell them that Jesus has appeared to Peter. Jesus then appears to them all. The Gospel ends with a short account of the 'Ascension' ('he led them out as far as Bethany, and, lifting up his hands, he blessed them. While he was blessing them, he withdrew from them and was carried up into heaven'), which seems to be placed on Easter Day here, rather than forty days later as in Acts 1.1–11. Luke includes more teaching by Jesus in his resurrection narratives than Matthew does. He interprets the scriptures to the two disciples on the way to Emmaus, and explains the prophecies that the Christ will suffer and rise on the third day, 'and that repentance and forgiveness of sins is to be proclaimed in his name to all nations, beginning from Jerusalem'. He instructs the disciples to stay in Jerusalem until they have been 'clothed with power from on high'. Another feature of the Lukan narratives is that two involve a meal (the meal at Emmaus has many features of the later eucharist, and Jesus is conceived as able to eat 'a piece of broiled fish' in front of the Eleven and their friends). And oddly, *two* 'men in dazzling apparel' appear suddenly to the women at the tomb and remind them of the predictions which Jesus made.

John

Two whole chapters in John's Gospel are given to the resurrection. It is here that we find the well-known story of Jesus' appearance to Mary Magdalene, the running of Peter and John to the tomb, and two appearances to the disciples in the upper room with the doors locked, a week apart. To Mary Jesus says that he has not yet ascended to the Father. In the first appearance in the upper room he breathes on the disciples and says, 'Receive the Holy Spirit. If you forgive the sins of any, they are forgiven them; if you retain the sins of any, they are retained,' while in the second he satisfies the doubts of Thomas, who then becomes the first person to address Jesus as 'My Lord and my God'. The familiar story of the disciples going back to Galilee to their fishing is told in what appears to be an appendix to the Gospel. Here Jesus addresses his question to Peter, 'Do you love me?', and prophesies that he will be imprisoned and put to death. Little of this is in the other Gospels.

Comment

I can remember my disappointment, as a small boy, with the risen Jesus. He did not seem to be the same as the Jesus in the earlier part of the Gospels. I did not know why then, but it now seems clear that the reason was that he is a more shadowy figure, appearing and disappearing, able to appear in a room where the doors were shut, and speaking in different ways from those before the crucifixion. Moreover, each of the writers of the Gospels not only tells the story in his own way, but makes Jesus speak in his own characteristic language. Whatever common tradition lies behind the narratives, and in whatever ways they are related, the evangelists have put their own imprint firmly on their writing. All four tell of women going to a tomb which is empty, but beyond that their accounts diverge markedly.

Frank Morison, in his famous book *Who Moved the Stone?*, argued that these are precisely the kind of differences which one would expect in the testimony of eye-witnesses, but as Christopher Evans has pointed out, such attempts to harmonize the traditions are really defeated from the start, for what we possess are not 'a number of scattered pieces from a single matrix' but four separate expressions of the Easter faith, each complete in itself. To take but one example. The risen Christ of Luke moves towards the ascension, but the Christ of Matthew stays with his followers until the end of the age. If, however, these are indeed expressions of the Easter faith, we need to consider what that faith is. But first we must turn to Paul.

Paul

The Gospels all describe the empty tomb. Paul seems unaware of this tradition, unless his reference to the burial of Jesus implies it. The resurrection lies at the heart of Paul's faith and preaching, yet when he refers to it he speaks of the appearances of the risen Christ – to Peter, to the 'Twelve', to more than five hundred 'brothers', to James (Jesus' brother), to 'all the apostles', and 'last of all' to himself (I Corinthians 15.3–8). The appearance to Paul is recounted three times in Acts (9.1–22; 22.4–16; 26.9–18) and once in Paul's own writings (Galatians 1.13–17). His own language suggests that he supposed that Christ's appearance to him was identical with the appearances to the earlier disciples whom he lists.

The first question to ask is whether Paul was right in this belief. There can be no certainty, and even if he were, this provides little evidence about the nature of the appearances that are described in the Gospels. Luke's account of the Damascus Road incident describes it in terms of a vision that was only partially seen by the bystanders, possibly not at all. But Paul may have interpreted it differently.

What is clear is that Paul refers to later visions which he had in different ways. He describes being caught up into the third heaven, but questions whether this was a purely spiritual experience (II Corinthians 12.1–4). Certainly he does not regard this as an 'appearance' of Jesus. Further, according to the account in Acts 22.17 Paul describes how Jesus appeared to him in a 'trance', which he seems to distinguish from the (resurrection) appearance of Jesus to him.

The second question is whether Paul knew the tradition of the empty tomb. As we have seen, 'buried' (I Corinthians 15.4) might imply this, for one may wonder how he understood the appearances to be those of the risen Christ if he supposed his body to be decaying in the tomb. We cannot know. What is clear is that, when he was trying to persuade the Christians at Corinth that those who had died would be raised to new life, he did not use the fact that the tomb was empty as a further proof that Jesus had been raised from the dead.

What form did the resurrection take?

The belief that Jesus really died and really rose from the dead dominates almost every book in the New Testament. Despite the doubts of Thomas and Matthew's comment that 'some doubted', the belief is firm and forms the ground of the life of the early church. The preacher on the resurrection (chapter 3), however, said that we must not be satisfied with an emotional faith. While he affirmed that he fully believed in the resurrection, and that Jesus is alive today, he accepted that Jesus' body had decayed like every other body.

The tradition of the empty tomb is firmly established, and it is not easy to offer convincing alternatives. Some claim that the body of Jesus would have been thrown into a common and unmarked grave with other criminals. There seems no reason to reject the Gospel narratives so completely, especially if Jesus had friends among the wealthy as well as among the poor. Indeed, the body of a man who had been crucified has been discovered by archaeologists. To suggest that the disciples actually did steal the body is incredible. Their future actions and their willingness to suffer for their beliefs make no sense on this supposition. It is possible, I suppose, that the Romans or the Jewish leaders disposed of the body to prevent the tomb becoming a place of pilgrimage and the centre of possible revolt, but there is no evidence for this – it is sheer conjecture.

More uncertain is the nature of the appearances. They may be thought of in three different ways.

First, the disciples may have 'seen' Jesus in exactly the same way that we 'see' other objects and people. In this case Jesus must be supposed to have 'materialized' in a physical form, such that anyone who was there would have seen him, and it would have been possible to take a photograph of him. He was not quite like ordinary persons in that he had the ability to materialize and vanish (so that appearing in a room with closed doors is no difficulty), but once he appeared he was as 'real' as any other object.

Second, we might think of the appearances as 'objective' visions, that is of visions of a real but spiritual being. In this case only those specially gifted or granted the ability by God would be able to 'see' the Jesus who was there all the time. The risen Christ is 'real', 'alive' and 'present', but not in a material form. This distinguishes these objective visions from the third possibility, that they were 'subjective' visions.

Subjective visions exist only in the mind of the person who has them. We might term them hallucinations, and like hallucinations they could be experienced by several people at the same time. This would not necessarily make the visions of Paul and the other disciples similar to the experiences of those recently bereaved persons, who tell us that they have seen their loved ones during the days after they died. They might be interpreted in terms of the surviving soul of Jesus communicating with the disciples through telepathy. Many who feel uneasy about experiences which are no more than an activity within the brain, may be ready to accept the idea of subjective visions if they are induced by a living Jesus. Others will hold that if the appearances of Jesus were no more than 'subjective' visions, this would destroy their faith that Jesus rose from the dead.

Conclusions

Scholars continue to debate these questions with undiminished enthusiasm, new books appearing every year – which probably shows that there are no easy answers. I end with the tentative speculation of one very eminent New Testament scholar.

C. F. D. Moule argues that a literal belief in the empty tomb might mean that the material of which Jesus' body was composed was somehow 'transformed' into a different mode of existence, somewhat in the same way that fuel is used up into energy. He distinguishes this from the Christian belief in what happens to human beings. Their bodies decompose, and he thinks it is inconceivable to entertain 'the bizarre idea . . . that the dissipated components of Christians long dead are, at the Last Day, to be reassembled so that they may be raised with the same bodies'. He wonders, however, whether it is conceivable that 'the total matter of this time-space existence is destined by the Creator not to be "scrapped" but to be used up into some other existence'. He suggests that this would mean that the difference between Christ and believers is 'only that Jesus *anticipates* their ultimate destiny'.

How far this is as 'ludicrous' as many later writers declare, and as Moule himself admits it may appear to be, is uncertain. Moule can find no alternative apart from abandoning the empty tomb or abandoning all suggestions about the nature of Jesus' resurrection. It brings us back to the issue we left aside at the beginning of this chapter: to what extent is the Christian belief in life after death dependent on an acceptance of the resurrection of Jesus?

The answer is far from obvious. Jesus and his disciples took life after death for granted. And when the church developed its doctrine on the future life it was the immortality of the soul that was affirmed. Indeed, it seems likely that the disciples spoke of the resurrection of Jesus because that was already part of their way of thought. In the New Testament, however, Paul and other writers link the resurrection of Jesus with that of believers, though rather by suggesting that he was a 'pioneer' going ahead of his brothers and sisters. So it is all part of a single belief in the reality of life after death.

Questions for discussion

1. Read through the resurrection narratives in the four Gospels. How do you react to the differences which have been pointed out in this chapter?

2. How has the discussion in this chapter affected your ideas about the resurrection?

3. Anne asked the preacher whether he could still sing the Easter hymns, and Fred accused him of not really believing that Jesus rose from the dead (chapter 3). What minimum belief do you think is necessary for a Christian to be able to say that he or she believes in the resurrection?

16

The Teaching of Jesus

Jesus predicted his death and resurrection more than once, according to the Gospels, but in this chapter we shall look at what he had to say about a future life.

This is not straightforward for three reasons. First, his teaching about individual life after death is closely bound up with the predictions he made about a future kingdom, possibly about the end of the world. Second, the best known teaching, such as 'In my Father's house are many mansions . . . if I go and prepare a place for you, I will come again and will take you to myself, so that where I am, there you may be also' and 'I am the resurrection and the life. Those who believe in me, even though they die, will live, and everyone who lives and believes in me will never die,' is found in John's Gospel, and many scholars today recognize that there is a large amount of interpretation in this Gospel. Indeed, some question whether any of the sayings of Jesus in John can be directly ascribed to Jesus. But third, even within the first three Gospels there is some doubt about the authenticity of the words of Jesus. We shall look at these in turn.

(a) In Mark 13 Jesus predicts wars and persecution. He declares that false messiahs will lead many astray. When his followers see 'the desolating sacrilege' set up they must escape to the mountains. It will be a time of great suffering. Then, after the sun is darkened, the moon turned into blood, and the stars fall from heaven, they will see 'the Son of Man coming in clouds'. He will send his angels to gather the chosen ones. Jesus adds that no one knows when this will happen. Only God the Father knows the time. Matthew and Luke have similar predictions, but they are absent from John.

The first thing to say about this chapter is that it resembles many such passages in Jewish writings from about the time of Jesus, known as apocalypses. Some of the imagery, such as the darkened sun and the blood-red moon, have been taken over from them, and possibly the term 'Son of Man' may come from apocalyptic writings as well. Two interpretations are current today. One is that Jesus was foretelling the end of the world and the setting up of an everlasting kingdom in heaven (or possibly on a renewed earth). The other is that Jesus and the Jews of his time regarded themselves as still being in exile from their homeland, and the picture language predicts the end of that exile, an end which arrived with the life, death and resurrection of Jesus. Plausible arguments can be put forward for both views. What is important for our present discussion of life after death is that the future life of the individual was closely linked with the future of the nation (or the church).

(b) The problem of the authenticity of the words of Jesus found only in John's Gospel is more delicate. Many devout Christians treasure these sayings and ground their faith upon them. Yet it has to be recognized that Jesus speaks differently in John from the way he expresses his teaching in the other Gospels, and that many of the things he says contain a very developed theology, probably the most advanced theology in the whole New Testament. I personally think that John was writing in much the same way that Plato wrote. Plato says that he is presenting a 'beautified' Socrates, and everyone accepts that many of the things that Socrates says in the dialogues are really the thoughts of Plato. John is writing theology rather than history, and many of the words that he puts into the mouth of Jesus are his own words. For this reason I shall restrict the account of the teaching of Jesus to the first three Gospels.

(c) Yet even in these Gospels some uncertainties remain. Matthew, for example, has more references to Gehenna than the other Gospels, and it may be that some of these come from Matthew rather than from Jesus himself. Scholars, indeed, are divided over whether Jesus ever threatened the wicked with everlasting punishment in Gehenna. Some accept that Jesus uttered some at least of these sayings, while others think that such threats are out of keeping with the character of Jesus and the main thrust of his teaching. We can never be sure. So far as we know, Jesus did not leave any writings; and, even if he did, the texts are lost. We have to depend, therefore, on memories of his teaching as collected and presented by the evangelists.

As we saw in the last chapter, Jesus took the existence of a life after death for granted, in just the same way that he took for granted many other beliefs that were common to the Jews of his day. He felt no need to present arguments for it, and when he spoke about it he used allusions that have been described as 'innocently unprecise' and 'intimations rather than descriptions'. We also need to remember that many different ideas about the end of the world and what happens after death were floating around in the time of Jesus (see chapter 14). It is no wonder, then, that, as Anne pointed out, the sayings of Jesus are somewhat inconsistent (chapter 7).

What, then, can we say with confidence about Jesus' own beliefs?

It is certain that he entertained no doubts at all about the existence of life after death. In answer to the Sadducees he quoted Exodus 3.6, 'I am the God of Abraham, and the God of Isaac, and the God of Jacob,' and interpreted this to mean that God remains the God of these three patriarchs and so they must still be alive, although they had died long ago. In the same debate with the Sadducees, however, Jesus declares that those who rise from the dead have a different form from their earthly existence. Like the angels, they do not marry. In his version of the incident Luke adds that those who have risen 'cannot die any more' and are 'sons of God, being sons of the resurrection' (Luke 20.27–38; Mark 12.18–27; Matthew 22.23–32).

In addition to including this debate with the Sadducees, Matthew recounts the parable of the sheep and the goats, where the Son of Man comes in his glory, and, in a judgment scene, the King separates those who are to inherit the kingdom prepared for them from the foundation of the world and are granted eternal life from those who are sent to eternal punishment (Matthew 25.31–46).

The most elaborate teaching in Luke is the story of the rich man and Lazarus, in which Lazarus, the beggar, is taken to 'Abraham's bosom', while the rich man is tormented by flames in Hades. In this story the rich man is able to see Lazarus, but a 'great chasm' is fixed between them (Luke 16.19–31). And on the cross Jesus says to one of the men crucified beside him, 'Truly I tell you, today you will be with me in Paradise' (Luke 23.43).

All these parables and sayings, however, use picture language. Both the parables speak of judgment, but in the Sheep and the Goats it takes place at the coming of the Son of Man, whereas in the Lukan parable it is implied that God has assessed the characters of the rich man and Lazarus during their lives. 'Paradise' in the saying from the cross derives from a Persian word meaning 'garden'. It came to refer to the place of future happiness for God's people. Again, the promise is that 'today' the criminal will be with Jesus in the happy afterlife. This fits in with the final word of Jesus according to Luke, 'Father, into your hands I commend my spirit' (Luke 23.43), a very different conclusion to the narrative of the crucifixion from that of Mark.

In addition to these passages there are the references to punishment of the wicked that Fred and Alec pointed to (chapter 6). Besides Mark 9.42–48 and its parallels in Matthew and Luke, there are references to Gehenna in Matthew 5.22, 29–30; 10.28; and 23.15. Gehenna, derived from the Hebrew name of the Valley of Hinnom where the refuse from Jerusalem was burned, became a term for future punishment. It is to be distinguished from Hades, the abode of the dead and the Greek equivalent of *sheol*, which is found in Matthew 11.23; 16.18; Luke 10.15; and 16.23. As we have noted, Matthew has many more references to Gehenna than the other Gospels, which casts some doubt on how central it was in the teaching of Jesus himself. Moreover, if Jesus did threaten the divine punishment of being destroyed 'both soul and body' in Gehenna (Matthew

83

10.28) this contrasts with the picture of the rich man apparently suffering permanent torment in the fire (Luke 16.23–25, 28).

When, however, we go on to ask what precisely Jesus believed, it is much more difficult to find a satisfactory answer. He definitely believed in a happy future with God for his followers (or, if we follow the parable in Matthew, those who perform deeds of kindness). Equally he accepted that there will be divine judgment. Whether the punishment is to be everlasting suffering or destruction in the fire is uncertain. And while on one occasion he expresses a belief in what we might call a 'spiritual' existence after death, on another occasion he speaks of 'soul and body' and seems to envisage the dead being raised in the body. If, therefore, we find ourselves confused about what will happen to us and our loved ones after death, we may perhaps find consolation in the fact that Jesus appears to have had no clear-cut picture of life after death either.

This may suggest that instead of being anxious to discover what life after death will be like we should, like Ron, simply put our trust in the love of the Father God. If God is the kind of God that Jesus believed in, then although what lies beyond death is shrouded in mystery, we can rely with absolute confidence on God, both for ourselves and for our loved ones. This, however, is unlikely to satisfy Mary and Anne, nor will Alec be content, though for different reasons.

Questions for discussion

1. Why do you think Mary, Anne and Alec will not be satisfied with the conclusions of this chapter?

2. To what extent, in your view, was Jesus a man of his own age when it came to thinking about life after death?

3. How do you think we should understand the parables that have been mentioned in this chapter?

17

The Rest of the New Testament

Throughout the New Testament we find confidence in life after death on the part of the leaders, though Paul shows that some Christians in Corinth had doubts. The expectations, however, are by no means uniform or consistent, and some think that Paul changed his mind during his lifetime. There is no space to discuss this in the same detail that we considered the resurrection and the teaching of Jesus. Instead I fasten on four issues.

The second coming and the end of the world
As with Jesus, the resurrection of individual Christians is not separated from the coming of Jesus and the end of the world. In I Corinthians, for example, Paul describes Jesus as the 'first fruits' – he is the first to be raised from the dead. Next he looks to his (second) coming, when those who have died will be raised to life. Then will come the end, when Christ hands over his authority to God the Father and will finally destroy death.

Other writings have a more developed scheme of events, the most elaborate being the Revelation to John, which is too complex to be considered in detail but which cannot be overlooked because it introduced into Christian thinking the ideas of the thousand-year reign of Christ after a first resurrection, a second resurrection to a final judgment, and the creation of a new heaven and a new earth, where death, mourning and pain are no more. This is symbolic language, much of it taken over from Jewish apocalypses, and it is impossible to say how far John thought that it was a literal picture of the future.

The most striking of the other references is I Thessalonians, perhaps the first of Paul's letters to be written. The Christians in Thessalonica were troubled because some of their friends had died and they wondered whether these friends would have lost out at the coming of Christ. Paul declares that Christ 'will descend from heaven, and the dead in Christ will rise first.' He expects that he himself will still be alive when Christ comes, for he continues: 'Then we who are alive, who are left, will be caught up in the clouds together with them to meet the Lord in the air; and so we will be with the Lord for ever.' There seems to be no reason to take this in any other way than literally. (An even more elaborate picture of the end of the world is presented in II Thessalonians, though some think the letter is not by Paul.) Even where there is no elaborate description of the end, Paul clearly still expects Christ to return and bring the present world to an end. There is no space to set out the evidence in detail and I simply point to Philippians 3.20; 4.6; Romans 13.11–14, where 'the day' is the day of Christ's coming; and some of the ethical teaching in I Corinthians, based on the assumption that the world will soon come to an end (see for example 7.25–31).

The resurrection

In I Thessalonians Paul simply describes the dead as being raised, presumably in the same form as they were before they died, since those Christians who are still alive will be caught up into heaven together with them.

By the time we come to I Corinthians he speaks of a 'resurrection body', which is different from the 'physical body' – as different as a plant is from the seed from which it comes. He declares that 'flesh and blood cannot inherit the kingdom of God', so that 'we will be changed, in a moment, in the twinkling of an eye, at the last trumpet' (I Corinthians 15.35–57). How exactly Paul envisaged this is uncertain. Probably he supposed that the Christian's body would be transformed, although some today find it easier to think of their 'personality' being 're-embodied' in a spiritual body. What is clear is that he did not believe in a crudely literal resurrection of dead bodies.

86

In II Corinthians 5.1–8 Paul's ideas appear to have developed even further. He contrasts our physical bodies ('the earthly tent') with a spiritual body ('a house not made with hands, eternal in the heavens'), and seems to hope that we may put on this 'spiritual body' over our physical bodies, rather like an overcoat, so that when we die our souls will still be 'dressed'. Whether Paul had come to adopt a belief in the 'soul' by this time is debated by scholars, but whether he had or not, he still thinks of some kind of 'body' being necessary for a full life, even though it is a 'spiritual' one.

If we are struggling to make sense of life after death, Paul is struggling too!

Judgment

The idea that God will judge everyone lies behind the whole theology of the New Testament. Salvation involves divine forgiveness and so deliverance from divine punishment. How this judgment was envisaged, however, is far from clear.

Again the Revelation to John contains the most elaborate picture. All the dead are raised in the second resurrection, and are judged by what is written in the books which record all their deeds. Anyone whose name is not written in the book of life will be thrown into the lake of fire (Revelation 20.11–15). Those written in the Lamb's book of life will live for ever in the light of God's presence. Although much of this is symbolic, the imagery has played an important part in popular ideas of life after death.

The other New Testament writers refer to God's judgment in far less specific ways. Paul speaks quite generally of God's judgment on sin in the first two chapters of his letter to the Romans, though he also refers to a coming 'day of wrath when God's righteous judgment will be revealed' and he will reward everyone according to what they have done (2.5, cf. 2.16). I Corinthians 3.10–15 shows that Paul certainly accepted the idea of a future judgment. For Christians, however, the verdict of acquittal is assured because they have based their lives on Christ. The beliefs of most of the other New Testament writers are similar. John refers to judgment on 'the last day' (John 12.48), yet in a sense the judgment is already taking place, for those who do not believe in Jesus are condemned already (3.18, cf. 5.24). The writer of the Letter to the Hebrews is similarly certain of future judgment, but he may perhaps think of it as immediately following death rather than at a future time (Hebrew 12.27).

Heaven and hell

We have already seen that the Revelation to John depicts the life of the redeemed as deathless, lived in the presence of God, in the new heaven and earth or in the new Jerusalem. None of the other New Testament writings have this amount of detail. John's Gospel speaks of 'eternal life' for those believing in Jesus, but the only specific mention of heaven is the famous saying about the many rooms in the Father's house, to which Jesus says he is going to prepare a place for his disciples and will come again to take them to be with him (John 14.2–3). Paul speaks generally about heaven, but primarily thinks of it as being in the presence of God (see II Corinthians 3.18).

Paul's reference to judgment implies that some will fail to enter heaven, but his emphasis is upon salvation and he rarely describes the fate of those who reject Christ. In Philippians 3.19 he says that the end of enemies of the cross will be 'destruction', and uses the same term in Romans 9.22. Twice he uses the strong term 'anathema' (I Corinthians 16.22; Galatians 1.9), which carries the idea of being accursed but does not necessarily involve being cast into an everlasting hell.

The writer of the Letter to the Hebrews speaks of 'fires of judgment' (10.27), and describes God as a 'consuming fire' (12.29). Apart from this, only Jude mentions eternal fire, while II Peter says that God cast the angels who sinned into 'hell' to await future judgment (2.4), but the word used is not the

Gehenna of the Gospels and in Greek thought referred to a place lower than Hades where punishment was meted out. It is striking that the most frequent references to 'hell' are in the teaching of Jesus as recorded in the first three Gospels, though, as we have seen, it is by no means certain that all (or any) of these go back to Jesus himself.

Summary

In this brief survey I have been unable even to touch on the difficulties in interpretation raised by all of these passages. Sufficient has been set out, however, to show that apart from the Revelation to John and the two letters to the Thessalonians, little interest in the *details* of life after death was shown by the first Christians. That Christ would come again, Christians (perhaps all the dead) would be raised, there would be a judgment, and those who were saved would enjoy life in the presence of God were assured beliefs. Beyond this, inquisitiveness seems to have been lacking.

Questions for discussion

1. Most, if not all, of the early Christians believed that Jesus would return soon to gather up his followers. It is now nearly 2000 years since the crucifixion. How do you think we should understand this belief?

2. The New Testament writers looked for a resurrection rather than immortality of the soul. In what ways should this influence our own beliefs?

3. What is your reaction to the lack of interest in detailed pictures of heaven and hell shown in most of the New Testament?

18

Christian Tradition

Christian thought after the time of the New Testament developed the ideas of the fate of those who had died. Ideas derived from the Revelation to John took on an importance because they alone filled in the details that were lacking in general beliefs in a future life lived with God. There was also the fact that Jesus had not come again, and this must have influenced ideas about the future both of the world and of individuals.

Official belief held that at the Last Day souls would reanimate their bodies and there would be a Grand Assize, after which they would be committed to heaven or hell, with the addition that those destined for heaven would first be purified in purgatory to make them fit to live in God's presence. Popular belief, however, appears to have placed the judgment at the time of death, so that death was immediately followed by going to heaven, possibly with an intermediate period in purgatory, or going to hell.

Thought about life after death, like many other areas of Western theology, was dominated by Augustine. He ridiculed the idea of the millennium, the thousand-year reign of Christ on earth, regarding it as a false interpretation of the Revelation. The 'first resurrection' was spiritual, experienced by baptized believers, so that the thousand years was the earthly life of the redeemed. (This idea led to some uneasiness as the year 1000 approached!) He accepted a literal resurrection, however, though he was aware of the difficulties involved in visualizing it. Moreover, he accepted that after the judgment the world would be consumed by fire and made into a new earth where the blessed would live for ever, while the wicked would be sent to everlasting torment. The scheme is depicted in many mediaeval paintings and is famously presented by Dante in the *Divine Comedy*.

Alongside this official teaching, with its horrific picture of everlasting torment, deliberately inflicted by the divine Judge, a belief in universal salvation is found from the time of the great scholar Origen in the third century. It was regarded as heretical, however, and in the nineteenth century Professor F. D. Maurice was forced out of his chair at King's College, London, because he rejected endless punishment in hell.

Perhaps a little more should be said about purgatory. During the Middle Ages the idea developed that those who committed minor sins, or those who had not been punished sufficiently during their lifetime, had to undergo a time of further punishment and cleansing before they could enter into God's presence. It then came to be believed that they could be assisted by our prayers (an idea that can be found in II Maccabees 12.39–45). In the fifteenth and sixteenth centuries masses for the dead became a major industry for the priests, and this, coupled with the selling of indulgences which were popularly thought to shorten the time that the dead had to spend in purgatory, provoked Luther to his first opposition to Rome. Some scholars have suggested that the idea could usefully be rehabilitated. John Hick, for example, argues that 'the gap between the individual's imperfection at the end of this life and the perfect heavenly state in which he is to participate has to be bridged'.

It will be seen that these traditional Christian beliefs assume that the individual lives on after death in essentially the same form as on earth. Indeed, it is difficult to imagine anything else. As Geoff pointed out on several occasions, a large part of our problems with thinking about life after death arise from a failure of imagination. This is perhaps why few descriptions of heaven are convincing. Eternal life is essentially static. This means that it lacks change and development, and the drive of purpose which is so important in terrestrial life is missing. Imagery tended to be treated literally, so that the worship of God in heaven was depicted as the endless singing of psalms and playing of harps! Only the greatest theologians, such as Thomas Aquinas, attempted to understand what the vision of God might mean.

This necessarily over-brief account of the 'four last things' – death, judgment, heaven and hell – points up the difficulties that Christians have had in trying to think their way beyond the death which comes to everyone. It also shows that the greatest problem for modern Christians who want to believe in life after death honestly and without embarrassment is the need to discover what survives of the individual rather than the simpler issues of judgment, heaven, and, more particularly, hell. Anne was probably right.

Questions for discussion

1. How do you envisage judgment?

2. John Hick thinks that some development of the individual to make him or her fit to experience God's immediate presence is a necessary part of any adequate view of life after death. What is your view of this?

3. What is your picture of heaven?

19

A Credible Belief?

Our rapid glance at the biblical evidence and traditional church teaching has brought us little closer to a solution to the problem of life after death. The reason is not far to seek. For the whole of the period that we have surveyed human beings were regarded as the special creation of God, made in his image. They were, therefore, held to be distinct from the rest of the natural world. Moreover, up to the second half of the nineteenth century it was assumed that life after death could be construed very much in terms of life on earth, despite ideas of the 'soul' as distinct from the body, or Paul's conception of the 'spiritual body'. Evolution and modern cosmology have changed all this, and the only way to reach a belief that can be held with confidence and not with a bad conscience is to start afresh.

It has to be said openly that the Bible offers little direct help. As we have seen, apart from one very late verse, the Old Testament view of life after death was of a shadowy existence in *sheol*, a land of darkness and forgetfulness, separate from fellowship with God. For all practical purposes death was regarded as the end. By the time of Jesus, belief in a resurrection was widespread, but it was thought of very literally by most people. Some continued to reject any hope of life beyond death, while a few took over Greek ideas of an immortal soul. Ideas were varied and inconsistent, however, and the only thing that can be said with any assurance is that Jesus and the first Christians were absolutely confident about life after death, although they used many different images to picture it. Only the Revelation to John presented a detailed scheme, and this proved a sadly misguided model for later generations of Christians. Too much attention was given to heaven and hell, when the nature of God and his love for human beings would have provided a more suitable foundation.

It will be necessary to reflect upon the nature of the universe and the place of human beings within the natural order before we can return to the central question of what persists after death.

Genesis 1–3 has exerted far too great an influence on Christian thought. We may feel that the writer who commented that it seems strange that members of the church should feel obliged to justify themselves by constant reference to 'the quasi-metaphysical speculations of a nomadic tribesman of the second millennium BC' went too far, and we may wish to retain these chapters for their poetic and spiritual meaning. Nevertheless, they have to be put firmly on one side if we are to arrive at a belief that can appear credible as we enter the twenty-first century.

While every scientific theory is open to revision, it seems reasonably certain that the universe evolved out of an initial unity of energy and matter, and that during the process of its evolution life appeared on the planet we inhabit. From this early form of life all the living beings, plants and animals, that we know today developed. Human beings are but one among the many species that evolved. Moreover, if we look to the future, life on this planet will come to an end when the sun ceases to be stable and expands to engulf the planets. Whether the entire universe will continue to expand until it reaches a cold equilibrium, or whether it will contract into its original unity is still debated, but either outcome will make it impossible for any life to survive.

It follows that the most convincing theologians and philosophers are those who seek to reinterpret the Christian faith in the light of these facts. Several things are clear. To conceive of God as 'maker' sets us off on the wrong track, since it retains the idea of a special creation. Rather we should think of him, following Ruth Page's suggestion, as 'letting possibility be'. This means that we can no longer conceive of God exercising a special providence, in which he takes unique care of human beings, but rather we must think of him as fully immersed within the universe as well as transcending it. The universe exists in God.

To develop these ideas is beyond the scope of this book, and another volume in the series will consider creation and providence. It is immediately important, however, to accept the kinship of humans with animals (and indeed with the rest of life on this earth), and the physical nature of their existence.

For some the conclusion follows that this life is all and death is the end. Personality cannot be separated from the physical body, and when that body ceases to function nothing remains but the elements of which it is composed. This, perhaps it needs to be emphasized, is not necessarily a non-Christian view, even though it goes against the whole of church tradition from New Testament times. Some who accept it would still wish to call themselves Christians. The strength of their position is that it fully recognizes the physical nature of human life and the links with the other forms of life on earth. Its weakness is that it hampers a faith in an omnipotent God who so loves the creatures that he has 'let it be possible' for them to evolve (to adapt Ruth Page's phrase). For we might wonder how such a God could be content to love them for a brief moment and then allow them to die. And, since belief in an all-loving God lies at the heart of the Christian religion, this is a serious weakness. It might be, of course, that by 'letting it be possible' for the universe to exist he also accepted the possibility that the life-span of living creatures would be limited. Most, however, will not be satisfied with this conclusion.

The idea that human beings possess an immortal soul has had a long and distinguished history. Again the weaknesses of the concept are obvious, though it is possible to overcome most of them. The main problem is to relate the soul to the body. Evolution makes this a particular difficulty. It might be supposed either that the soul is inherited from the parents with the body or that God creates the soul individually.

(The theory, going back to Origen, that souls are pre-existent has never been widely accepted in Christian circles.) The second of these suppositions can hardly be entertained, given the view of the relation of God to the universe that has been accepted here, while the first falters at the attempt to determine at which point in the course of evolution souls first came into existence. But perhaps to think in this way is to imagine the soul in too physical a way, as if it were a 'body', though of a different kind. If it is conceived as 'personality', it becomes just possible to retain the idea. Nevertheless, the difficulties in interpreting personality in ways that make possible its existence apart from the body are formidable, and with some reluctance we may conclude that there is little future in this approach.

Resurrection has become popular in recent years, partly owing to the view that it represents biblical teaching, partly because it is seen fully to accept the death of the individual and so to accord more nearly with medical and biological theory. It is curious to find some scholars defending the idea on the basis of Hebrew psychology, which for most of the Old Testament involved the acceptance of the finality of death. And in any case other features of Hebrew psychology would not be preferred to modern scientific theory. New Testament teaching on resurrection, as we have seen, ranges from the crudely literal to the highly sophisticated. Only Paul's idea of a 'spiritual body' merits serious consideration. It requires a special intervention of God, and for some this will be questionable. Moreover, even those who find no difficulty in 'special interventions' still have to wrestle with the idea, already considered, of the resurrected individual as a 'replica'. Only on the assumption that the 'replica' possesses memory will he or she have no doubt about their identity and for all purposes *be* the original individual. And if any aspect of that individual is held to be carried over, we are dealing with a 'soul' theory, with all its intrinsic problems.

Both immortal 'soul' or 'personality' and 'resurrection' have been championed by learned scholars and neither can be lightly dismissed. In spite of this, we may feel that both approaches ultimately fail because they assume too close a similarity between this life and the next. Time, for example, is an aspect of the present universe. God, and eternity, are without time. When the present universe 'ends', time will cease to exist. Such facts have persuaded some scholars that any hope of presenting a convincing idea of life after death must be a radical departure from earlier, pre-evolutionary, conceptions.

We have already considered the proposal put forward by John Macquarrie. Here we offer suggestions by Ruth Page and John Polkinghorne.

Ruth Page asks, 'Can companionship with God ever end?' and answers her question by affirming that the only basis of hope beyond death lies in trust in the eternal love of God. She interprets 'salvation' as 'the discovery that a relationship with God already exists; that one is already befriended, judged, forgiven; that a continuing mutual relationship has been made possible by God's initiative, within which human belief and action may respond to divine encouragement, reproof or consolation; and that this synergy or concurrence is always possible between the human and the divine'. She then extends this 'concurrence' to the non-human world and argues that it all becomes part of God's positive experience and so cannot be lost. How far this is different from our future life being simply a memory in the mind of God might be doubted, especially as Ruth Page admits that we may wonder how far we remain ourselves in all this – and is rather dismissive of the desire.

The mathematical physicist, John Polkinghorne, offers a slightly different proposal. He begins by asserting that 'one way or the other, the universe is condemned to ultimate futility, and humanity will prove to have been a transient episode in its history,' thus rightly linking the fate of the individual with that of the universe. Like Ruth Page, he grounds his belief in God's faithfulness and his care for his creatures, which will not allow anything that is good to be lost. Polkinghorne claims that his belief is in a resurrection, not in the survival of a spiritual component of the human being, but his idea of resurrection is far removed from those which have been considered so far. He holds that the psychosomatic unity that forms a human being is dissolved at death, but 'the pattern that is me' is remembered by God and will be recreated by him 'in a new environment of his choosing'. He accepts as 'a very crude and inadequate analogy' the computer image of 'the software running on our present hardware' being 'transferred to the hardware of the world to come', presumably along the lines that the 'program' which is our personality is taken from our 'floppy disk' (our body) into the computer's memory (God) and then copied on the new floppy disk (the resurrection body) within the future universe. And this future world involves 'cosmic redemption'. The analogy is 'crude and inadequate' because the whole present universe is already in the mind of God, and, as we have seen, it is in any case essentially a 'soul' hypothesis. Its virtue is that it accepts the futility of the present universe and relates life after death closely to it, so that animals could be included in it, though, he thinks, as species rather than as individuals, and he leaves open the question of pets! We might wonder why the whole universe, including all the animals, might not share in the 'cosmic redemption'. This last idea, however, is not without its own difficulty. If, as Polkinghorne believes, we shall meet our loved ones again beyond the grave, then our future life must be remarkably similar to the present one – and we might wonder whether the similarities extend to time and space.

The last sentence leads us to the next chapter.

Questions for discussion

1. Why, do you think, most Christians are unwilling to accept that death is the end?

2. Consider the arguments in favour of an immortal soul and the resurrection of the body. Which do you find more persuasive?

3. Discuss your reaction to the hypotheses of Ruth Page and John Polkinghorne.

20

Other Important Matters

Why do we have so great a concern about life after death? One reason, certainly, is our own fear of death and our inability to conceive of a time when we shall simply 'not be here'. More important for most of us, however, is the fear of final separation from our loved ones. Death seems to say, 'Never again' – never again shall we see that beloved face, hear that well-known voice, touch that hand, kiss those lips. Is it really possible that one day we shall meet our loved ones again?

In their discussions several of the friends found it very difficult to conceive of a future life in which this was possible. As Mary realized (chapter 4), we all change and our relationships change, so that we are not the persons we were ten, twenty, fifty, seventy years ago. How will it be possible to relate to people who had died long before we did? Thus even if the redeemed universe was sufficiently similar to our own to make recognition possible, it would be a different kind of relationship. Geoff hinted that, granted the limits of our imagination, we can do no more than leave our loved ones in the hand of God and trust in his goodness and love. It may well be that this is indeed as far as we can go.

One dominant strand in Christian thinking places the believer's vision of God and fellowship with him at the centre of ideas of heaven. Some will no doubt regard this as self-centred, as well as unfeeling, yet there is without doubt an important truth here. If it is anything, the future life must be life with God – and perhaps life in God. Certainly, this gives a right understanding of the meaning of hell. Hell, far from being a place of everlasting torture, is being deprived of that vision of God and fellowship with him.

Two other matters that were mentioned by the friends need to be picked up, if only briefly.

100

The first is Mrs Smith's comment about the unfairness of the present world and her demand that things should be set right in the world after death. This, it will be recalled, may have been one of the main reasons why belief in a resurrection finally appeared among the Jews. They saw those who were faithful to God being martyred while their oppressors enjoyed happiness and success, and they looked to a time when all would receive their just deserts. And it was, after all, the main argument the great philosopher Immanuel Kant put forward for the existence of a future life. Life certainly is unfair – not just in the way that 'rewards' and 'punishments' are meted out to the individual, but in the way that place of birth largely determines the quality of a person's life – and perhaps a just God should be expected to apportion pleasure and suffering. Even if we reject the use of hell as a threat to ensure compliance with socially acceptable behaviour, we can still see that there is something in the idea of future reward. Some moralists, on the other hand, will argue that punishment and reward have no place in the highest morality, and some philosophers suggest that this world is 'a vale of soul making' so that the suffering is not to be regarded as 'punishment' or the comforts as 'reward'. Nevertheless, we have to face the fact that many millions are crushed by their suffering, which can in no way be seen as a means of developing their personalities. Even if we find it difficult to go along with Kant, most will probably hope that the joys of heaven will in some measure compensate for the pains suffered on earth. Or are we now reverting to inadequate and defective ideas of what is involved in an intelligible view of the after-life?

Anne mentioned her Hindu colleague who believed in reincarnation. Interest in the idea has been aroused by current knowledge of eastern religions, and many people have become aware of the belief through features in the media. It is too large an issue to consider in any depth, but a few points may be made.

Reincarnation has never been an orthodox Christian belief, and four main objections to it are usually put forward. (1) It is not found in the New Testament. (2) Christianity attributes absolute importance to this present life as the time when our eternal salvation (or damnation) is determined. The seriousness of our decision for Christ would be undermined if we had further opportunities to make the choice in future lives. (3) It is at variance with the doctrine of the resurrection of the body. (4) The fact that Christ's sacrifice is regarded in the New Testament as once-for-all makes reincarnation impossible for human beings. In addition it might be pointed out that Indian religions look for an eventual release from the round of rebirths, so that reincarnation is only a stage in the life of the individual and a final, eternal, state is still desired.

For many the first will be decisive. Others may question whether the New Testament evidence forbids it as a possible option. As for the second argument, believers in reincarnation hold that it is unfair that our eternal destiny should depend upon a single lifetime – but this can be countered by some form of the purgatory belief. The third is far from obvious, since the individual might be 'resurrected' into a new life on earth instead of as a 'spiritual body'. The final argument is hardly cogent, since a once-for-all incarnation and atonement could be effective for everyone in their multiple incarnations.

Reincarnation is sometimes defended on the grounds that some people have claimed to recall incidents in their previous existence. Since most of the examples come from societies where reincarnation is an accepted belief, the evidence is not without the danger of bias, and so far it cannot be said that solid proof has been forthcoming.

It is true that reincarnation would help to solve the problem of the unfairness of life, since in Indian philosophy the law of *karma* works through successive births. To be fully effective, however, it would seem to require a memory of previous holy or sinful lives, which is lacking. And in any case, the problem of unjust suffering is only thrown back to the previous life, then to the one before that, and so on till the first 'incarnation' in reached.

'Archie's "funeral"' raises two important issues which need to be set out more systematically than in the discussion.

In the first place, it directs our attention to the connections between animals and human beings in the chain of being. Both have evolved, and, in many ways, human beings are only superior animals. We have seen that one of the difficulties with the concept of an immortal soul is to determine at what point in evolution early human beings developed souls (or, on the less convincing form of the theory, at what point God began to create souls and join them to the human beings). On a resurrection hypothesis there seem to be no grounds, apart from human pride, for supposing that animals will not also be raised from the dead. The more probable theories of Page and Polkinghorne would seem to contain no bar to the continuation of the life of all creatures in the mind of God: indeed, Page's proposal favours it.

We saw that Anne's comment that Mrs Marsh's dog was more of a friend to her than a baby which died on the day it was born raised a horrified objection from Mary. Moreover, hospital chaplains tell us of the bond between parents and babies and even foetuses in miscarriages, and of consequent requests not just for Christian burial but even for baptism in some cases. Yet it seems to be undeniable that our personalities develop through our relations with other people, and this must raise questions about ideas of a soul which is treated as 'grown-up' even when the dead person is a very young baby. The questions that came to Mary and Anne in the cemetery will not readily go away.

Near-death experiences were considered fairly fully by the friends, but a further comment may still be in order. Those who have studied such experiences point out the marked similarities between many of the accounts – feelings of peace and joy, out of the body experience, a dark tunnel at the end of which is a light, the barrier between the individual and the light, visiting another country, meeting friends and relatives, reviewing one's life, the moment of realizing that one must 'go back', the vivid memory of the experience, which does not necessarily lead to religious conversion but often makes a difference to the way one lives and usually takes away all fear of death. These experiences are clearly compatible with belief in the soul, but less obviously with a doctrine of resurrection. Since, however, the person who had them did not actually *die*, they are always open to the explanation that they were produced by a combination of expectations derived from society and physical factors, such as lowered blood pressure and loss of blood to the brain. No more than the claims of spiritualist mediums do they provide any firm proof that the individual personality survives death.

Conclusion

The path we have trodden must seem remarkably stony. In the end we have been forced to concede that to accept the finality of death is simpler than any belief in a future life. Nevertheless, ideas of a soul which survives the death of the body and of a resurrection to a new kind of life have not been ruled out of court. On the whole, however, a belief in our life 'held' in some way in God seems to accord better with the modern understanding of the universe. This is not entirely a comfortable faith, since it does not present any vivid picture of life in heaven with our loved ones, but this may only be a failure of imagination. Its main strength lies in its close conformity with the wider eschatology of the end of the universe.

There is one thing more to say, and it is the most important of all. Faith here may be faltering, and reason may have reached the end of its ability to understand. What is left is the God who, so the Christian believes, revealed himself through Jesus of

Nazareth as a loving Father. Where we cannot see we can only trust. When our imagination fails we must stay silent. But it is a silence in the presence of that loving Father.

Questions for discussion

1. Consider whether life after death really solves the problem of the unfairness of life.

2. If you know any Hindus, ask them about reincarnation and *karma*. Is it only prejudice which makes us reject these ideas?

3. What are your own thoughts and feelings as you come to the end of this book?

Further Reading

These suggestions for further reading are arranged by topics and according to importance or accessibility.

Three books that deal specifically with life after death are:

John Hick, *Death and Eternal Life*, Collins 1976, ISBN 0-00-215157-X.

This is a comprehensive survey of the field, including contributions from eastern religions. Clearly written, though some of the ideas are difficult. The present book is greatly indebted to this study.

Paul Badham, *Christian Beliefs about Life after Death*, Macmillan 1976, ISBN 0-333-19769-0.

This is notable for its defence of the concept of the soul and its immortality. It also considers (and rejects) the alternative idea of resurrection, holding that it depends for its validity upon some concept of the soul.

Hans Küng, *Eternal Life?*, Collins 1984, reissued SCM Press 1991, ISBN 0-334-02519-2.

Written with Küng's usual clarity and verve, this important work is perhaps of less immediate appeal to English readers because it is set against the background of continental philosophy, especially Feuerbach, Marx, and the existentialists.

Books which range more widely but include important discussions of individual survival are:

Ruth Page, *God and the Web of Creation*, SCM Press 1996, ISBN 0-334-02653-9.

Although only the last six pages are devoted to life after death, this is an important book because it takes modern cosmology and biology seriously and offers a genuine alternative to traditional beliefs.

John Polkinghorne, *Science and Christian Belief: Theological reflections of a bottom-up thinker*, SPCK 1994, ISBN 0-281-04714-6.

In the work Polkinghorne takes the reader through the Nicene Creed. Chapter 9, 'We look for the resurrection of the dead, and the life of the world to come', is valuable because it sets the belief within the 'ultimate futility' of the universe.

John Macquarrie, *Christian Hope*, Mowbrays 1978, ISBN 0-264-66064-1.

This is a widely ranging study by a leading theologian, in the concluding chapter of which he discusses the destiny of the individual. Earlier in the book he considers eschatology and the second coming of Christ.

Two studies on particular themes are:

Jonathan L. Kvanvig, *The Problem of Hell*, Oxford University Press 1993, ISBN 0-19-508487-X.

Kvanvig examines a number of views of hell, and argues that any adequate view must be rooted in the character of God. He accepts without question or debate the certainty of life for the individual after death.

Is There Life After Death?

Richard Swinburne, *The Evolution of the Soul*, Clarendon Press, Oxford, revd edn 1997, ISBN 0-19-823698-0.

Swinburne is a strong defender of the existence of the soul, and this revised edition of his book takes into account the latest discussion. Importantly, he accepts the full implications of evolution. Only the final chapter considers the future of the soul after death. Swinburne writes with remorseless logic, and although the argument is always clear it demands close attention.

Most of the general introductions to the Philosophy of Religion contain a chapter on life after death. One of the clearest is:

David A. Pailin, *Groundwork of Philosophy of Religion*, Epworth Press 1986, ISBN 0-7162-0418-5.

In Chapter 9, 'Faith, Death and Immortality', Pailin deals with 'Puzzles of post-mortem existence', 'subjective immortality' (i.e. that individuals continue as self-conscious persons after death) and 'objective immortality' (i.e. that individuals' experiences are 'preserved' in God's awareness).

Many recent books deal with caring for the dying and the bereaved, but are less concerned with problems of life after death. One recent study deals more fully with theology:

Geoff Walters, *Why Do Christians Find It Hard to Grieve?*, Paternoster Press 1997, ISBN 0-85364-787-9.

Walters argues that many Christians find it hard to cope with grief because they feel that they ought to believe in the immortality of the soul. This, however, is a Greek not a biblical belief. A resurrection faith accepts the reality of death and so opens up the way to 'healthy grieving'.

References

p. ix I owe this schoolgirl's poem to Raymond Short, who read it in a school magazine. The author is unknown.

p. 15 The lines are from Laurence Binyon's 'For the Fallen'.

p. 22 These words from a sermon by E. B. Pusey are quoted by John Hick, *Death and Eternal Life*, Collins 1976, p. 200.

p. 53 Plato, *The Last Days of Socrates*, trs. Hugh Tredennick, Penguin 1954, p. 113.
Plato, *Protagoras and Meno*, trs. W. K. C. Guthrie, Penguin 1956, pp. 130–38.

p. 54 G. Ryle, *The Concept of Mind*, Hutchinson 1949, is probably the most influential attack on Cartesian dualism. Antony Flew, *Body, Mind and Death*, Macmillan 1964, p. 28, sees Ryle as emancipating us from 'the beguiling errors of Descartes'.
H. D. Lewis discusses the soul in his *Philosophy of Religion*, English Universities Press 1965, pp. 273–88. Paul Badham rejects the idea of resurrection and champions the soul in *Christian Beliefs about Life after Death*, Macmillan 1976. Richard Swinburne strongly defends the concept of the soul in *The Evolution of the Soul*, OUP 1986, revd edn 1997.

p. 55 H. D. Lewis examines the phrase in his *Philosophy of Religion*, p. 277.

p. 57 *Doctrine in the Church of England*, SPCK 1936, p. 209.

p. 59 John Hick, *Death and Eternal Life*, pp. 278–96.

p. 61 John Macquarrie, *Christian Hope*, Mowbrays 1978, pp. 112–27. Jacques Pohier gives an account of his personal quest for understanding in *God – in Fragments*, SCM Press 1985. His earlier book that was regarded as heretical was *Quand je dis Dieu* (1977).

p. 73 *The Apocryphal New Testament*, ed. J. K. Elliott, Clarendon Press, Oxford 1993, pp. 156–57.

p. 75 Frank Morison, *Who Moved the Stone?*, Faber & Faber 1958; Christopher Evans, *Resurrection and the New Testament*, SCM Press 1970, p. 128.

p. 78 C. F. D. Moule (ed.), *The Significance of the Message of the Resurrection for Faith in Jesus Christ*, SCM Press 1968, pp. 9–11.

p. 91 John Hick, *Death and Eternal Life*, p. 202.

p. 94 The writer referred to is I. Ball, 'Sing an Old-fashioned Song' in I. Ball, M. Goodall, C. Palmer and J. Reader (eds), *The Earth Beneath: A Critical Guide to Green Theology*, SPCK 1992, p. 125.

The idea of God's 'letting possibility be' runs through Ruth Page's *God and the Web of Creation*, SCM Press 1996; she expounds the idea in the first part and examines the consequences in the second.

p. 97 Ruth Page, *God and the Web of Creation*, p. 169.

John Polkinghorne, *Science and Belief: Theological reflections of a bottom-up thinker*, SPCK 1994, pp. 162–64. The whole chapter on 'Eschatology' is important for his overall view of 'cosmic redemption'.